Switching to Angular 2

Build SEO-friendly, high-performance single-page
applications with Angular 2

This book is based on RC4

Minko Gechev

PUBLISHING

BIRMINGHAM - MUMBAI

Switching to Angular 2

First published: March 2016

Production reference: 2020816

Published by Packt Publishing Ltd.
Livery Place
35 Livery Street
Birmingham B3 2PB, UK.

ISBN 978-1-78588-620-1

www.packtpub.com

Credits

Author
Minko Gechev

Reviewers
Miško Hevery
Daniel Lamb

Commissioning Editor
Edward Gordon

Acquisition Editor
Kirk D'costa

Content Development Editor
Shweta Pant

Technical Editor
Mohita Vyas

Copy Editor
Akshata Lobo

Project Coordinator
Kinjal Bari

Proofreader
Safis Editing

Indexer
Mariammal Chettiyar

Graphics
Disha Haria

Production Coordinator
Nilesh Mohite

Cover Work
Nilesh Mohite

Foreword

Angular 2 is still Angular, just better. It is still built on the same principles that made you love AngularJS: a quick and powerful solution to building Single Page Applications. In Angular 2, the applications are faster, more visible to SEO and mobile, and are cross-platform ready. So whilst Angular 2 has improved many of the concepts over AngularJS, the philosophy remains true to the original vision.

Switching to Angular 2 is a book that recognizes this. Minko's book successfully helps you to switch your thinking from AngularJS 1.x to Angular 2. From your first interactions with Angular 2 to the last, the core concepts of Angular are maintained throughout. This guide will help you to switch to Angular's new way of doing things. Minko guides you through the changes and new features that have been introduced—components, directives, TypeScript, the new router, and everything else you need to start using Angular 2 for your next project.

As Angular 2 takes up the challenge set by today's changing web development landscape and builds on the legacy of AngularJS, it's incredibly important for the Angular community that there are high quality learning materials such as Minko's book to help Angular developers make that first switch over to the future.

Miško Hevery

Creator of AngularJS and Angular 2

About the Author

Minko Gechev is a software engineer who strongly believes in open source software. He has developed numerous such projects, including AngularJS 1.x and Angular 2 style guides, angular2-seed, a static code analyzer for Angular 2 projects, aspect.js, angular-aop, and many others. He runs training courses in JavaScript, Angular, and other web technologies.

Minko loves to experiment with theoretical concepts from computer science and apply them in practice. He has spoken about Angular and software development at worldwide conferences and meetups, including ng-conf, ng-vegas, AngularConnect, ITWeekend Kiev, AngularJS-SF, and Angular Berlin.

I want to thank Miško Hevery for his great contributions in software engineering and the technical review of this book. He helped me provide as precise content as possible. To make the code samples for the book easy to run, I used angular2-seed. Core contributor of the project is Ludovic Hénin, who helped make it much more than an Angular 2 starter. I also want to thank to Daniel Lamb, Radoslav Kirov and Tero Parviainen who gave me extremely valuable feedback!

I couldn't complete the book without the dedicated work of the Packt Publishing team.

Finally, I want to thank the team at Google for giving us Angular. They are a constant inspiration.

About the Reviewers

Miško Hevery is the creator of the AngularJS framework. He has a passion for making complex things simple. He currently works at Google, but has previously worked at Adobe, Sun Microsystems, Intel, and Xerox, where he became an expert in building web applications in web-related technologies, such as Java, JavaScript, Flex, and ActionScript.

Daniel Lamb is a senior software development professional and an author who enjoys sharing the knowledge he has gained, specializing in large-scale architecture and frontend web development. His work over the last 16 years has enabled hundreds of millions to engage and interact during billions of visits.

www.PacktPub.com

eBooks, discount offers, and more

Did you know that Packt offers eBook versions of every book published, with PDF and ePub files available? You can upgrade to the eBook version at www.PacktPub. com and as a print book customer, you are entitled to a discount on the eBook copy. Get in touch with us at customercare@packtpub.com for more details.

At www.PacktPub.com, you can also read a collection of free technical articles, sign up for a range of free newsletters and receive exclusive discounts and offers on Packt books and eBooks.

https://www2.packtpub.com/books/subscription/packtlib

Do you need instant solutions to your IT questions? PacktLib is Packt's online digital book library. Here, you can search, access, and read Packt's entire library of books.

Why subscribe?

- Fully searchable across every book published by Packt
- Copy and paste, print, and bookmark content
- On demand and accessible via a web browser

Table of Contents

Preface

AngularJS is a JavaScript development framework that makes building web applications easier. It is used today in large-scale, high-traffic websites that struggle with underperformance and portability issues, as well as SEO unfriendliness and complexity at scale. Angular 2 changes these.

It is the modern framework you need to build performant and robust web applications. *Switching to Angular 2* is the quickest way to get to grips with Angular 2, and it will help you transition into the brave new world of Angular 2.

By the end of the book, you'll be ready to start building quick and efficient Angular 2 applications that take advantage of all the new features on offer.

What this book covers

Chapter 1, Getting started with Angular 2, kicks off our journey into the world of Angular 2. It describes the main reasons behind the design decisions of the framework. We will look into the two main drivers behind the shape of the framework—the current state of the Web and the evolution of frontend development.

Chapter 2, The Building Blocks of an Angular 2 Application, gives an overview of the core concepts introduced by Angular 2. We'll explore how the foundational building blocks for the development of applications provided by AngularJS 1.x differ from the ones in the last major version of the framework.

Chapter 3, TypeScript Crash Course, explains that although Angular 2 is language agnostic, Google's recommendation is to take advantage of the static typing of TypeScript. In this chapter, you'll learn all the essential syntax you need to develop Angular 2 applications in TypeScript!

Chapter 4, Getting Started with Angular 2 Components and Directives, describes the core building blocks for developing the user interface of our applications—directives and components. We will dive into concepts such as view encapsulation, content projection, inputs and outputs, change detection strategies, and more. We'll discuss advanced topics such as template references and speeding up our applications using immutable data.

Chapter 5, Dependency Injection in Angular 2, covers one of the most powerful features in the framework, which was initially introduced by AngularJS 1.x: its dependency injection mechanism. It allows us to write more maintainable, testable, and understandable code. By the end of this chapter, we will know how to define the business logic in services and glue them together with the UI through the DI mechanism. We will also look into some more advanced concepts, such as the injectors hierarchy, configuring providers, and more.

Chapter 6, Working with the Angular 2 Router and Forms, explores the new module for managing forms in the process of developing a real-life application. We will also implement a page that shows the entered through the form data. In the end, we will glue the individual pages together into an application by using the component-based router.

Chapter 7, Explaining Pipes and Communicating with RESTful services, dives into the router and the forms modules in detail. Here, we will explore how we can develop model-driven forms and define parameterized and child routes. We will also explain the HTTP module and see how we can develop pure and impure pipes.

Chapter 8, SEO and Angular 2 in the Real World, explores some advanced topics in the Angular 2 application development, such as running an application in Web Workers and server-side rendering. In the second part of the chapter, we will explore tools that can ease our daily life as developers, such as `angular-cli`, and `angular2-seed`, explain the concept of hot reloading, and more.

What you need for this book

All you need to work through most of the examples in this book is a simple text editor or an IDE, Node.js, TypeScript installed, Internet access, and a browser. The examples in the book are tested on Google Chrome 51+ but they should work in all popular browsers supported by Angular 2.

Each chapter introduces the software requirements for running the provided snippets.

Who this book is for

Do you want to jump in at the deep end of Angular 2? Or perhaps you're interested in assessing the changes before moving over? If so, then *Switching to Angular 2* is the book for you.

To get the most out of the book, you'll need to have basic understanding of AngularJS 1.x and have a good understanding of JavaScript. No knowledge of the changes made to Angular 2 is required to follow along.

Conventions

In this book, you will find a number of text styles that distinguish between different kinds of information. Here are some examples of these styles and an explanation of their meaning.

Code words in text, database table names, folder names, filenames, file extensions, pathnames, dummy URLs, user input, and Twitter handles are shown as follows: "You should see the same result, but without the test.js file stored on the disk."

A block of code is set as follows:

```
@Injectable()
class Socket {
  constructor(private buffer: Buffer) {}
}

let injector = ReflectiveInjector.resolveAndCreate([
  { provide: BUFFER_SIZE, useValue: 42 },
  Buffer,
  Socket
]);


injector.get(Socket);
```

When we wish to draw your attention to a particular part of a code block, the relevant lines or items are set in bold:

```
let injector = ReflectiveInjector.resolveAndCreate([
  { provide: BUFFER_SIZE, useValue: 42 },
  Buffer,
  Socket
]);
```

Each code snippet which is in the repository with the code from this book starts with a comment with its corresponding file location, relative to the app directory:

```
// ch5/ts/injector-basics/forward-ref.ts

@Injectable()
class Socket {
  constructor(private buffer: Buffer) {…}
}
```

New terms and **important words** are shown in bold. Words that you see on the screen, for example, in menus or dialog boxes, appear in the text like this: "When the markup is rendered onto the screen, all that the user will see is the label: **Loading....**"

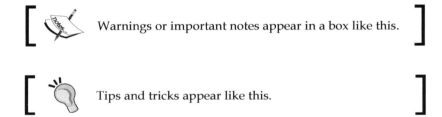

Warnings or important notes appear in a box like this.

Tips and tricks appear like this.

Reader feedback

Feedback from our readers is always welcome. Let us know what you think about this book—what you liked or disliked. Reader feedback is important for us as it helps us develop titles that you will really get the most out of.

To send us general feedback, simply e-mail feedback@packtpub.com, and mention the book's title in the subject of your message.

If there is a topic that you have expertise in and you are interested in either writing or contributing to a book, see our author guide at www.packtpub.com/authors.

Customer support

Now that you are the proud owner of a Packt book, we have a number of things to help you to get the most from your purchase.

Downloading the example code

You can download the example code files for this book from GitHub at `https://github.com/mgechev/switching-to-angular2`.

You can download the code files by following these steps:

1. Enter the URL in your browser's address bar.
2. Click on the "Download ZIP" button located in the mid-right part of the screen.

You can also download the example code files for this book from your account at `http://www.packtpub.com`. If you purchased this book elsewhere, you can visit `http://www.packtpub.com/support` and register to have the files e-mailed directly to you.

You can also download the code files by following these steps:

1. Log in or register to our website using your e-mail address and password.
2. Hover the mouse pointer on the **SUPPORT** tab at the top.
3. Click on **Code Downloads & Errata**.
4. Enter the name of the book in the **Search** box.
5. Select the book for which you're looking to download the code files.
6. Choose from the drop-down menu where you purchased this book from.
7. Click on **Code Download**.

Once the file is downloaded, please make sure that you unzip or extract the folder using the latest version of:

- WinRAR / 7-Zip for Windows
- Zipeg / iZip / UnRarX for Mac
- 7-Zip / PeaZip for Linux
- Chapters 3 and 4 contain further information for the installation process.

Errata

Although we have taken every care to ensure the accuracy of our content, mistakes do happen. If you find a mistake in one of our books—maybe a mistake in the text or the code—we would be grateful if you could report this to us. By doing so, you can save other readers from frustration and help us improve subsequent versions of this book. If you find any errata, please report them by visiting http://www.packtpub. com/submit-errata, selecting your book, clicking on the **Errata Submission Form** link, and entering the details of your errata. Once your errata are verified, your submission will be accepted and the errata will be uploaded to our website or added to any list of existing errata under the Errata section of that title.

To view the previously submitted errata, go to https://www.packtpub.com/books/ content/support and enter the name of the book in the search field. The required information will appear under the **Errata** section.

Piracy

Piracy of copyrighted material on the Internet is an ongoing problem across all media. At Packt, we take the protection of our copyright and licenses very seriously. If you come across any illegal copies of our works in any form on the Internet, please provide us with the location address or website name immediately so that we can pursue a remedy.

Please contact us at copyright@packtpub.com with a link to the suspected pirated material.

We appreciate your help in protecting our authors and our ability to bring you valuable content.

Questions

If you have a problem with any aspect of this book, you can contact us at questions@packtpub.com, and we will do our best to address the problem.

1
Getting Started with Angular 2

On September 18, 2014, the first public commit was pushed to the Angular 2 repository. A few weeks later, at **ng-europe**, Igor and Tobias from the core team gave a short overview of what Angular 2 was expected to be. The vision at that time was far from final; however, one thing was certain—the new version of the framework would be entirely different from AngularJS 1.x.

This announcement brought a lot of questions and controversy. The reasons behind the drastic changes were quite clear—AngularJS 1.x was no longer able to take full advantage of the evolved Web and to completely satisfy the requirements of large-scale JavaScript applications. A new framework would let Angular developers capitalize on developments in web technology in simpler and more direct ways. Yet, people were concerned. One of the biggest nightmares with backward incompatibility for developers is the migration of their current codebases to the new version of the third-party software they use. In Angular's case, after that first announcement, migration looked daunting, even impossible. Later, at **ng-conf** 2015 and **ng-vegas**, different migration strategies were introduced. The Angular community came together and shared additional ideas, anticipating the benefits of Angular 2 while preserving the things learned from AngularJS 1.x.

This book is a part of that project. Making the upgrade to Angular 2 is non-trivial, but it is worth it. The main drivers behind the drastic changes in Angular 2 and its lack of backward compatibility are the evolution of the Web, and the lessons learned from the usage of AngularJS 1.x in the wild. Switching to Angular 2 will help you to learn the new framework by understanding how we got here and why Angular's new features make intuitive sense for the modern Web in building high-performance, scalable, single-page applications.

The evolution of the Web – time for a new framework

In the last couple of years, the Web has evolved in big steps. During the implementation of ECMAScript 5, the ECMAScript 6 standard started its development (now known as **ECMAScript 2015** or **ES2015**). ES2015 introduced many changes in the language such as adding built-in language support for modules, block scope variable definition, and a lot of syntactical sugar, such as classes and destructuring.

Meanwhile, **Web Components** were invented. Web Components allow us to define custom HTML elements and attach behavior to them. Since it is hard to extend the existing HTML elements with new ones (such as dialogs, charts, grids, and more) mostly because of the time required for consolidation and standardization of their APIs, a better solution is to allow developers to extend the existing elements the way they want. Web Components provide us with a number of benefits, including better encapsulation, better semantics of the markup we produce, better modularity, and easier communication between developers and designers.

We know that JavaScript is a single-threaded language. Initially, it was developed for simple client-side scripting, but over time, its role has shifted quite a bit. Now with HTML5, we have different APIs that allow audio and video processing, communication with external services through a two-directional communication channel, transferring and processing big chunks of raw data, and more. All these heavy computations in the main thread may create a poor user experience. They may introduce freezing of the user interface when time-consuming computations are being performed. This led to the development of **WebWorkers**, which allow the execution of the scripts in the background that communicate with the main thread through message passing. This way, multi-threaded programming has been brought to the browser.

Some of these APIs were introduced after the development of AngularJS 1.x had begun; that's why the framework wasn't build with most of them in mind. However, exploiting the APIs gives developers many benefits, such as:

- Significant performance improvements.
- Development of software with better quality characteristics.

Now let's briefly discuss how each of these technologies has been made part of the new Angular core and why.

The evolution of ECMAScript

Nowadays, browser vendors are releasing new features in short iterations, and users receive updates quite often. This helps move the Web forward by allowing developers to take advantage of the bleeding-edge technologies, aiming to improve the Web. ES2015 is already standardized. The implementation of the latest version of the language has already started in the major browsers. Learning the new syntax and taking advantage of it will not only increase our productivity as developers, but also prepare us for the near future when all the browsers will have full support for it. This makes it essential to start using the latest syntax now.

Some projects' requirements may enforce us to support older browsers, which does not support any ES2015 features. In this case, we can directly write ECMAScript 5, which has different syntax but equivalent semantics to ES2015. However, we can take advantage of the process of **transpilation**. Using a transpiler in our build process allows us to take advantage of the new syntax by writing ES2015 and translating it to a target language that is supported by the browsers.

AngularJS has been around since 2009. Back then, the frontend of most websites was powered by ECMAScript 3, the last main release of ECMAScript prior to ECMAScript 5. This automatically meant that the language used for the framework's implementation was ECMAScript 3. Taking advantage of the new version of the language requires porting of the entirety of AngularJS 1.x to ES2015.

From the beginning, Angular 2 took into account the current state of the Web by bringing the latest syntax in the framework. Although Angular 2 is written with a superset of ES2016 (TypeScript, which we're going to take a look at in a moment), it allows developers to use language of their own preference. We can use ES2015 or, if we prefer not to have any intermediate preprocessing of our code and simplify the build process, even ECMAScript 5.

Web Components

The first public draft of Web Components was published on May 22, 2012, about three years after the release of AngularJS 1.x. As mentioned, the Web Components standard allows us to create custom elements and attach behavior to them. It sounds familiar; we've already used similar concept in the development of the user interface in AngularJS 1.x applications. Web Components sound like an alternative to Angular directives; however, they have more intuitive API, richer functionality, and built-in browser support. They introduced a few other benefits such as better encapsulation, which is very important, for example, in handling CSS-style collisions.

A possible strategy for adding Web Components support in AngularJS 1.x is to change the directives implementation and introduce primitives of the new standard in the DOM compiler. As Angular developers, we know how powerful but also complex the directives API is. It includes a lot of properties such as `postLink`, `preLink`, `compile`, `restrict`, `scope`, `controller`, and many more, and of course, our favorite `transclude`. Approved as standard, Web Components will be implemented on a much lower level in the browsers, which introduces plenty of benefits such as better performance and native API.

During the implementation of Web Components, a lot of web specialists met the same problems the Angular team did when developing the directives API and came up with similar ideas. Good design decisions behind Web Components include the **content** element, which deals with the infamous transclusion problem in AngularJS 1.x. Since both the directives API and Web Components solve similar problems in different ways, keeping the directives API on top of Web Components would have been redundant and added unnecessary complexity. That's why the Angular core team decided to start from the beginning by building on top of Web Components and taking full advantage of the new standard. Web Components involves new features, some of them not yet implemented by all browsers. In case our application is run in a browser, which does not support any of these features natively, Angular 2 emulates them. An example for this is the content element polyfilled with the directive, `ng-content`.

WebWorkers

JavaScript is known for its event loop. Usually JavaScript programs are executed in a single thread and different events are scheduled by being pushed in a queue and processed sequentially, in the order of their arrival. However, this computational strategy is not effective when one of the scheduled events requires a lot of computational time. In such cases the event's handling is going to block the main thread and all other events are not going to be handled until the time consuming computation is complete and passes the execution to the next one in the queue. A simple example of this is a mouse click that triggers an event, in which callback we do some audio processing using the HTML5 audio API. If the processed audio track is big and the algorithm running over it is heavy, this will affect the user's experience by freezing the UI until the execution is complete.

The WebWorker API was introduced in order to prevent such pitfalls. It allows execution of heavy computations inside the context of different thread, which leaves the main thread of execution free, capable of handling user input and rendering the user interface.

How can we take advantage of this in Angular? In order to answer this question, let's think about how things work in AngularJS 1.x. What if we have an enterprise application, which processes a huge amount of data that needs to be rendered on the screen using data binding? For each binding, a new watcher will be added. Once the digest loop is run, it will loop over all the watchers, execute the expressions associated with them, and compare the returned results with the results gained from the previous iteration. We have a few slowdowns here:

- The iteration over large number of watchers.
- Evaluation of expression in given context.
- Copy of the returned result.
- Comparison between the current result of the expression's evaluation and the previous one.

All these steps could be quite slow depending on the size of the input. If the digest loop involves heavy computations, why not move it to a WebWorker? Why not run the digest loop inside WebWorker, get the changed bindings, and apply them to the DOM?

There were experiments by the community, which aimed for this result. However, their integration into the framework wasn't trivial. One of the main reasons behind the lack of satisfying results was the coupling of the framework with the DOM. Often, inside the watchers' callbacks, Angular directly manipulates the DOM, which makes it impossible to move the watchers inside WebWorkers since the WebWorkers are invoked in an isolated context, without access to the DOM. In AngularJS 1.x, we may have implicit or explicit dependencies between the different watchers, which require multiple iterations of the digest loop in order to get stable results. Combining the last two points, it is quite hard to achieve practical results in calculating the changes in threads other than the main thread of execution.

Fixing this in AngularJS 1.x introduces a great deal of complexity in the internal implementation. The framework simply was not built with this in mind. Since WebWorkers were introduced before the Angular 2 design process started, the core team took them in mind from the beginning.

Lessons learned from AngularJS 1.x in the wild

Although the previous section introduced a lot of arguments for the required reimplementation of the framework responding to the latest trends, it's important to remember that we're not starting completely from scratch. We're taking what we've learned from AngularJS 1.x with us. In the period since 2009, the Web is not the only thing that evolved. We also started building more and more complex applications. Today, single-page applications are not something exotic, but more like a strict requirement for all the web applications solving business problems, which are aiming for high performance and good user experience.

AngularJS 1.x helped us to build highly-efficient and large-scale single-page applications. However, by applying it in various use cases, we've also discovered some of its pitfalls. Learning from the community's experience, Angular's core team worked on new ideas aiming to answer the new requirements. As we look at the new features of Angular 2, let's consider them in the light of the current implementation of AngularJS 1.x and think about the things with which we, as Angular developers, have struggled and which we have modified over the last few years.

Controllers

AngularJS 1.x follows the **Model View Controller** (**MVC**) micro-architectural pattern. Some may argue that it looks more like **Model View ViewModel** (**MVVM**) because of the view model attached as properties to the scope or the current context in case of controller as syntax. It could be approached differently again if we use the **Model View Presenter pattern** (**MVP**). Because of all the different variations of how we can structure the logic in our applications the core team called AngularJS 1.x a **Model View Whatever** (**MVW**) framework.

The view in any AngularJS application is supposed to be a composition of directives. The directives collaborate together in order to deliver fully functional user interfaces. Services are responsible for encapsulating the business logic of the applications. That's the place where we should put the communication with RESTful services through HTTP, real-time communication with WebSockets and even WebRTC. Services are the building block where we should implement the domain models and business rules of our applications. There's one more component, which is mostly responsible for handling user input and delegating the execution to the services — the controller.

Although the services and directives have well-defined roles, we can often see the anti-pattern of the **Massive View Controller**, which is common in iOS applications. Occasionally, developers are tempted to access or even manipulate the DOM directly from their controllers. Initially, this happens for achieving something simple, such as changing the size of an element, or quick and dirty changing elements' styles. Another noticeable anti-pattern is duplication of business logic across controllers. Often developers tend to copy and paste logic, which should be encapsulated inside services.

The best practices for building AngularJS applications state is that the controllers should not manipulate the DOM at all, instead all DOM access and manipulations should be isolated in directives. If we have some repetitive logic between controllers, most likely we want to encapsulate it into a service and inject this service with the dependency injection mechanism of AngularJS in all the controllers that need that functionality.

This is where we're coming from in AngularJS 1.x. All this said, it seems that the functionality of controllers could be moved into the directive's controllers. Since directives support the dependency injection API, after receiving the user's input, we can directly delegate the execution to a specific service, already injected. This is the main reason Angular 2 uses a different approach by removing the ability to put controllers everywhere by using the ng-controller directive. We'll take a look at how AngularJS 1.x controllers' responsibilities could be taken from Angular 2 components and directives in *Chapter 4, Getting Started with Angular 2 Components and Directives*.

Scope

The data-binding in AngularJS is achieved using the scope object. We can attach properties to it and explicitly declare in the template that we want to bind to these properties (one or two-way). Although the idea of the scope seems clear, the scope has two more responsibilities, including event dispatching and the change detection-related behavior. Angular beginners have a hard time understanding what scope really is and how it should be used. AngularJS 1.2 introduced something called **controller as syntax**. It allows us to add properties to the current context inside the given controller (this), instead of explicitly injecting the scope object and later adding properties to it. This simplified syntax can be demonstrated from the following snippet:

```
<div ng-controller="MainCtrl as main">
  <button ng-click="main.clicked()">Click</button>
</div>
```

```
function MainCtrl() {
  this.name = 'Foobar';
}
MainCtrl.prototype.clicked = function () {
  alert('You clicked me!');
};
```

Angular 2 took this even further by removing the `scope` object. All the expressions are evaluated in the context of given UI component. Removing the entire scope API introduces higher simplicity; we don't need to explicitly inject it anymore and we add properties to the UI components to which we can later bind. This API feels much simpler and more natural.

We're going to take more detailed look at the components and the change detection mechanism of Angular 2 in *Chapter 4*, *Getting Started with Angular 2 Components and Directives*.

Dependency Injection

Maybe the first framework on the market that included **inversion of control (IoC)** through **dependency injection (DI)** in the JavaScript world was AngularJS 1.x. DI provides a number of benefits, such as easier testability, better code organization and modularization, and simplicity. Although the DI in 1.x does an amazing job, Angular 2 takes this even further. Since Angular 2 is on top of the latest web standards, it uses the ECMAScript 2016 decorators' syntax for annotating the code for using DI. Decorators are quite similar to the decorators in Python or annotations in Java. They allow us to *decorate* the behavior of a given object by using reflection. Since decorators are not yet standardized and supported by major browsers, their usage requires an intermediate transpilation step; however, if you don't want to take it, you can directly write a little bit more verbose code with ECMAScript 5 syntax and achieve the same semantics.

The new DI is much more flexible and feature-rich. It also fixes some of the pitfalls of AngularJS 1.x such as the different APIs; in 1.x, some objects are injected by position (such as the scope, element, attributes, and controller in the directives' link function) and others, by name (using parameters names in controllers, directives, services, and filters).

We will take a further look at the Angular 2's dependency injection API in *Chapter 5*, *Dependency Injection in Angular 2*.

Server-side rendering

The bigger the requirements of the Web are, the more complex the web applications become. Building a real-life, single-page application requires writing a huge amount of JavaScript, and including all the required external libraries may increase the size of the scripts on our page to a few megabytes. The initialization of the application may take up to several seconds or even tens of seconds on mobile until all the resources get fetched from the server, the JavaScript is parsed and executed, the page gets rendered, and all the styles are applied. On low-end mobile devices that use a mobile Internet connection, this process may make the users give up on visiting our application. Although there are a few practices that speed up this process, in complex applications, there's no silver bullet.

In the process of trying to improve the user experience, developers discovered something called **server-side rendering**. It allows us to render the requested view of a single-page application on the server and directly provide the HTML for the page to the user. Later, once all the resources are processed, the event listeners and bindings can be added by the script files. This sounds like a good way to boost the performance of our application. One of the pioneers in this was ReactJS, which allowed pre-rendering of the user interface on the server side using Node.js DOM implementations. Unfortunately, the architecture of AngularJS 1.x does not allow this. The showstopper is the strong coupling between the framework and the browser APIs, the same issue we had in running the change detection in WebWorkers.

Another typical use case for the server-side rendering is for building **Search Engine Optimization (SEO)**-friendly applications. There were a couple of hacks used in the past for making the AngularJS 1.x applications indexable by the search engines. One such practice, for instance, is traversal of the application with a headless browser, which executes the scripts on each page and caches the rendered output into HTML files, making it accessible by the search engines.

Although this workaround for building SEO-friendly applications works, server-side rendering solves both of the mentioned issues, improving the user experience and allowing us to build SEO-friendly applications much more easily and far more elegantly.

The decoupling of Angular 2 with the DOM allows us to run our Angular 2 applications outside the context of the browser. The community took advantage of this by building a tool, allowing us to prerender the views of our single-page application on the server side and forward them to the browser. At the time of writing the following content, the tool is still in the early phases of its development and is outside the framework's core. We're going to take a further look at it in *Chapter 8*, *Development Experience and Server-Side Rendering*.

Applications that scale

MVW has been the default choice for building single-page applications since Backbone.js appeared. It allows separation of concerns by isolating the business logic from the view, allowing us to build well-designed applications. Exploiting the observer pattern, MVW allows listening for model changes in the view and updating it when changes are detected. However, there are some explicit and implicit dependencies between these event handlers, which make the dataflow in our applications not obvious and hard to reason about. In AngularJS 1.x, we are allowed to have dependencies between the different watchers, which requires the digest loop to iterate over all of them a couple of times until the expressions' results get stable. Angular 2 makes the data-flow one-directional, which has a number of benefits, including:

- More explicit data-flow.
- No dependencies between bindings, so no **time to live (TTL)** of the digest.
- Better performance:
    - The digest loop is run only once.
    - We can create apps, which are friendly to immutable/observable models, that allows us to make further optimizations.

The change in the data-flow introduces one more fundamental change in AngularJS 1.x architecture.

We may take another perspective on this problem when we need to maintain a large codebase written in JavaScript. Although JavaScript's duck typing makes the language quite flexible, it also makes its analysis and support by IDEs and text editors harder. Refactoring of large projects gets very hard and error-prone because in most cases, the static analysis and type inference are impossible. The lack of compiler makes typos all too easy, which are hard to notice until we run our test suite or run the application.

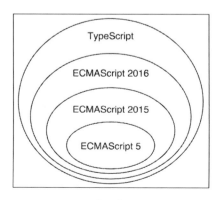

The Angular core team decided to use TypeScript because of the better tooling possible with it and the compile-time type checking, which help us be more productive and less error-prone. As the preceding figure shows, TypeScript is a superset of ECMAScript; it introduces explicit type annotations and a compiler. The TypeScript language is compiled to plain JavaScript, supported by today's browsers. Since version 1.6, TypeScript implements the ECMAScript 2016 decorators, which makes it the perfect choice for Angular 2.

The usage of TypeScript allows much better IDE and text editors support with static code analysis and type checking. All this increases our productivity dramatically by reducing the mistakes we make and simplifying the refactoring process. Another important benefit of TypeScript is the performance improvement we implicitly get by the static typing, which allows run-time optimizations by the JavaScript virtual machine.

We'll be talking about TypeScript in detail in *Chapter 3, TypeScript Crash Course*.

Templates

Templates are one of the key features in AngularJS 1.x. They are simple HTML and do not require any intermediate processing and compilation, unlike most template engines such as mustache. Templates in AngularJS combine simplicity with power by allowing us to extend HTML by creating an internal **Domain Specific Language (DSL)** inside it, with custom elements and attributes.

However, this is one of the main purposes behind web components as well. We already mentioned how and why Angular 2 takes advantage of this new technology. Although AngularJS 1.x templates are great, they can still get better! Angular 2 templates took the best parts of the ones in the previous release of the framework and enhanced them by fixing some of their confusing parts.

For example, let's say we built a directive and we want to allow the user to pass a property to it by using an attribute. In AngularJS 1.x, we can approach this in three different ways:

```
<user name="literal"></user>
<user name="expression"></user>
<user name="{{interpolate}}"></user>
```

If we have a directive `user` and we want to pass the `name` property, we can approach in three different ways. We can either pass a literal (in this case, the string `"literal"`), a string, which will be evaluated as an expression (in our case `"expression"`), or an expression inside `{{ }}`. Which syntax should be used completely depends on the directive's implementation, which makes its API-tangled and hard to remember.

It is a frustrating task to deal with large amount of components with different design decisions on a daily basis. By introducing a common convention, we can deal with such problems. However, in order to have good results and consistent APIs, the entire community needs to agree with it.

Angular 2 deals with this problem as well by providing special syntax for attributes, whose values need to be evaluated in the context of the current component, and a different syntax for passing literals.

Another thing we're used to, based on our AngularJS 1.x experience, is the microsyntax used in template directives such as `ng-if`, `ng-for`. For instance, if we want to iterate over a list of users and display their names in AngularJS 1.x, we can use:

```
<div ng-for="user in users">{{user.name}}</div>
```

Although this syntax looks intuitive to us, it allows limited tooling support. However, Angular 2 approached this differently by bringing a little bit more explicit syntax with richer semantics:

```
<template ngFor let-user [ngForOf]="users">
  {{user.name}}
</template>
```

The preceding snippet explicitly defines the property, which has to be created in the context of the current iteration (`user`), the one we iterate over (`users`).

However, this syntax is too verbose for typing. Developers can use the following syntax, which later gets translated to the more verbose one:

```
<li *ngFor="let user of users">
  {{user.name}}
</li>
```

The improvements in the new templates will also allow better tooling for advanced support by text editors and IDEs. We're going to discuss Angular 2's templates in *Chapter 4, Getting Started with Angular 2 Components and Directives*.

Change detection

In the *WebWorkers* section, we already mentioned the opportunity to run the digest loop in the context of a different thread, instantiated as WebWorker. However, the implementation of the digest loop in AngularJS 1.x is not quite memory-efficient and prevents the JavaScript virtual machine from doing further code optimizations, which allows significant performance improvements. One such optimization is the inline caching (`http://mrale.ph/blog/2012/06/03/explaining-js-vms-in-js-inline-caches.html`). The Angular team did a lot of research discovering different ways the performance and the efficiency of the digest loop could be improved. This led to the development of a brand new change detection mechanism.

In order to allow further flexibility, the Angular team abstracted the change detection and decoupled its implementation from the framework's core. This allowed the development of different change detection strategies, empowering different features in different environments.

As a result, Angular 2 has two built-in change detection mechanisms:

- **Dynamic change detection**: This is similar to the change detection mechanism used by AngularJS 1.x. It is used in systems with disallowed `eval()`, such as CSP and Chrome extensions.
- **JIT change detection**: This generates the code that performs the change detection run-time, allowing the JavaScript virtual machine to perform further code optimizations.

We're going to take a look at the new change detection mechanisms and how we can configure them in *Chapter 4, Getting Started with Angular 2 Components and Directives*.

Summary

In this chapter, we considered the main reasons behind the decisions taken by the Angular core team and the lack of backward compatibility between the last two major versions of the framework. We saw that these decisions were fueled by two things—the evolution of the Web and the evolution of the frontend development, with the lessons learned from the development of AngularJS 1.x applications.

In the first section, we learned why we need to use the latest version of the JavaScript language, why we want to take advantage of Web Components and WebWorkers, and why it's not worth it to integrate all these powerful tools in version 1.x.

We observed the current direction of frontend development and the lessons learned in the last few years. We described why the controller and scope were removed from Angular 2, and why AngularJS 1.x's architecture was changed in order to allow server-side rendering for SEO-friendly, high-performance, single-page applications. Another fundamental topic we took a look at was building large-scale applications, and how that motivated single-way data-flow in the framework and the choice of the statically-typed language TypeScript.

In the next chapter, we're going to look at the main building blocks of an Angular 2 application—how they can be used and how they relate to each other. Angular 2 reuses some of the naming of the components introduced by AngularJS 1.x, but generally changes the building blocks of our single-page applications completely. We're going to peek at the new components, and compare them with the ones in the previous version of the framework. We'll make a quick introduction to directives, components, routers, pipes, and services, and describe how they could be combined for building classy, single-page applications.

Downloading the example code

You can download the example code files for this book from your account at http://www.packtpub.com. If you purchased this book elsewhere, you can visit http://www.packtpub.com/support and register to have the files e-mailed directly to you.

You can download the code files by following these steps:

- Log in or register to our website using your e-mail address and password.
- Hover the mouse pointer on the **SUPPORT** tab at the top.
- Click on **Code Downloads & Errata**.
- Enter the name of the book in the **Search** box.
- Select the book for which you're looking to download the code files.
- Choose from the drop-down menu where you purchased this book from.
- Click on **Code Download**.

Once the file is downloaded, please make sure that you unzip or extract the folder using the latest version of:

- WinRAR / 7-Zip for Windows
- Zipeg / iZip / UnRarX for Mac
- 7-Zip / PeaZip for Linux

2
The Building Blocks of an Angular 2 Application

In the previous chapter, we looked at the drivers for the design decisions behind Angular 2. We described the main reasons that led to the development of a brand new framework; Angular 2 takes advantage of web standards while keeping the past lessons in mind. Although we are familiar with the main drivers, we still haven't described the core Angular 2 concepts. The last major release of the framework took a different path from AngularJS 1.x and introduced a lot of changes in the fundamental building blocks used for the development of single-page applications.

In this chapter, we'll look at the framework's core and make a brief introduction to the main components of Angular 2. Another important purpose of this chapter is to take an overview of how these concepts can be put together to help us build professional user interfaces for our web applications. The following sections will give us an overview of everything that we are going to take a look at in more detail later in the book.

In this chapter, we're going to look at:

- A conceptual overview of the framework, showing how different concepts relate to each other.
- How we can build a user interface as a composition of components.
- What path the directives took in Angular 2, and how their interface changed compared to the previous major version of the framework.
- The reasons for the enforced separation of concerns, which led to the decomposition of the directives into two different components. In order to get better sense of these two concepts, we're going to demonstrate basic syntax for their definition.

- An overview of the improved change detection, and how it involves the context that directives provide.
- What zones are, and why they can make our daily development process easier.
- What pipes are, and how are they related to the AngularJS 1.x filters.
- The brand-new **dependency injection (DI)** mechanism in Angular 2 and how it is related to the service component.

A conceptual overview of Angular 2

Before we dive into different parts of Angular 2, let's get a conceptual overview of how everything fits together. Let's have a look at the following diagram:

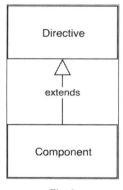

Fig. 1

Fig. 1 to *Fig. 4* shows the main Angular 2 concepts and the connections between them. The main purpose of these diagrams is to illustrate the core blocks for building single-page applications with Angular 2, and their relations.

The **Component** is the main building block we're going to use to create the user interface of our applications with Angular 2. The Component is a direct successor of the Directive, which is the primitive for attaching behavior to the DOM. Components extend **Directives** by providing further features, such as a view with an attached template, which can be used for rendering composition of directives. Inside the template of the view can reside different expressions.

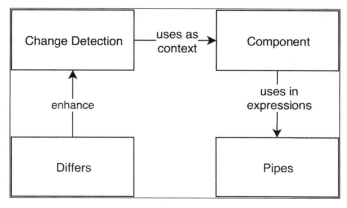

Fig. 2

The preceding diagram illustrates conceptually the **Change Detection** mechanism of Angular 2. It runs the `digest` loop, which evaluates the registered expressions in the context of specific UI components. Since the concept of scope has been removed from Angular 2, the execution context of the expressions are the controllers of the components associated with them.

The **Change Detection** mechanism can be enhanced using **Differs**; that's why there's a direct relation between these two elements on the diagram.

Pipes are another component of Angular 2. We can think of the Pipes as the filters from AngularJS 1.x. Pipes can be used together with components. We can include them in the expressions, which are defined in the context of any component:

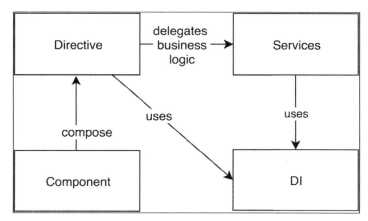

Fig. 3

Now let's take a look at the preceding diagram. **Directives** and **Components** delegate the business logic to **Services**. This enforces better separation of concerns, maintainability, and reusability of code. **Directives** receive references to instances of specific services declared as dependencies using the **DI** mechanism of the framework, and delegate the execution of the business related logic to them. Both **Directives** and **Components** may use the **DI** mechanism, not only to inject services, but also to inject DOM elements and/or other **Components** or **Directives**.

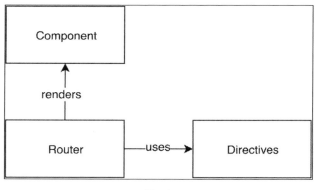

Fig. 4

Lastly, the component-based router is used for defining the routes in our application. Since **Directives** do not own a template, only the **Components** can be rendered by the router, representing the different views in our application. The router also uses the predefined directives, which allow us to define hyperlinks between the different views and the container where they should be rendered.

Now we're going to look more closely at these concepts, see how they work together to make Angular 2 applications, and how they've changed from their AngularJS 1.x predecessors.

Changing directives

AngularJS 1.x introduced the concept of directives in the development of single-page applications. The purpose of directives is to encapsulate the DOM-related logic, and allow us to build user interfaces as compositions of such components by extending the syntax and the semantics of HTML. Initially, like most innovative concepts, directives were viewed controversially because they predispose us to write invalid HTML when using custom elements or attributes without the `data-` prefix. However, over time, this concept has gradually been accepted, and has proved that it is here to stay.

Another drawback of the implementation of directives in AngularJS 1.x are the different ways we can use them. This requires understanding of the attribute values, which can be literals, expressions, callbacks, or microsyntax. This makes tooling essentially impossible.

Angular 2 keeps the concept of directives, but takes the best parts from AngularJS 1.x and adds some new ideas and syntax. The main purpose of Angular 2's directives is to attach behavior to the DOM by extending it with custom logic defined in an ES2015 class. We can think of these classes as controllers associated to the directives, and think of their constructors as similar to the linking function of the directives from AngularJS 1.x. However, the new directives have limited configurability. They do not allow for the definition of a template, which makes most of the already known properties for defining directives unnecessary. The simplicity of the directives API does not limit their behavior, but only enforces stronger separation of concerns. To complement this more simple directive API, Angular 2 has introduced a richer interface for the definition of UI elements, called components. Components extend the functionality of directives by allowing them to own a template, through the Component metadata. We're going to take a further look at components later.

The syntax used for Angular 2 directives involves ES2016 decorators. However, we can also use TypeScript, ES2015, or even **ECMAScript** 5 (**ES5**) in order to achieve the same result with a little bit more typing. The following code defines a simple directive, written in TypeScript:

```
@Directive({
  selector: '[tooltip]'
})
export class Tooltip {
  private overlay: Overlay;
  @Input() private tooltip: string;
  constructor(private el: ElementRef, manager: OverlayManager) {
    this.overlay = manager.get();
  }
  @HostListener('mouseenter')
  onMouseEnter() {
    this.overlay.open(this.el.nativeElement, this.tooltip);
  }
  @HostListener('mouseleave')
  onMouseLeave() {
    this.overlay.close();
  }
}
```

The directive can be used with the following markup in our template:

```
<div tooltip="42">Tell me the answer!</div>
```

Once the user points over the the label, `Tell me the answer!`, Angular will invoke the method, defined under the `@HostListener` decorator in the directive's definition. In the end, the open method of the overlay manager will be executed. Since we can have multiple directives on a single element, the best practices state that we should use an attribute as a selector.

An alternative ECMAScript 5 syntax for the definition of this directive is:

```
var Tooltip = ng.core.Directive({
  selector: '[tooltip]',
  inputs: ['tooltip'],
  host: {
    '(mouseenter)': 'onMouseEnter()',
    '(mouseleave)': 'onMouseLeave()'
  }
})
.Class({
  constructor: [ng.core.ElementRef, Overlay, function (tooltip, el,
manager) {
    this.el = el;
    this.overlay = manager.get();
  }],
  onMouseEnter() {
    this.overlay.open(this.el.nativeElement, this.tooltip);
  },
  onMouseLeave() {
    this.overlay.close();
  }
});
```

The preceding ES5 syntax demonstrates the internal JavaScript **Domain Specific Language (DSL)** that Angular 2 provides in order to allow us to write our code without the syntax, which is not yet supported by modern browsers.

We can summarize that Angular 2 has kept the concept of directives by maintaining the idea of attaching behavior to the DOM. The core differences between 1.x and 2 are the new syntax, and the further separation of concerns introduced by bringing the components. In *Chapter 4, Getting Started with Angular 2 Components and Directives*, we will take a further look at directives' API. We'll also compare the directives' definition syntax using ES2016 and ES5. Now let's have a look at the big change to Angular 2 components.

Getting to know Angular 2 components

Model View Controller (MVC) is a micro-architectural pattern initially introduced for the implementation of user interfaces. As AngularJS developers, we use different variations of this pattern on a daily basis, most often **Model View ViewModel (MVVM)**. In MVC, we have the model, which encapsulates the business logic of our application, and the view, which is responsible for rendering the user interface, accepting user input, as well as delegating the user interaction logic to the controller. The view is represented as the composition of components, which is formally known as the **composite design pattern**.

Let's take a look at the following structural diagram, which shows the composite design pattern:

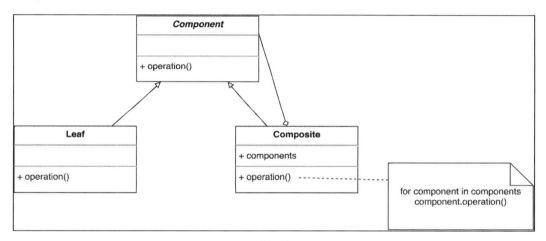

Fig. 5

Here we have three classes:

- An abstract class called Component.
- Two concrete classes called Leaf and Composite. The Leaf class is a simple terminal component in the component tree that we're going to build soon.

The Component class defines an abstract operation called operation. Both Leaf and Composite inherit from the Component class. However, the Composite class also owns references to it. We can take this even further and allow Composite to own a list of references to Component instances, as shown in the diagram. The components list inside Composite can hold references to different Composite or Leaf instances, or instances of other classes, which extend the Component class or any of its successors. In the implementation of the method, operation, inside Composite, the invoked operation of the different instances inside the loop can behave differently. This is because of the late binding mechanism used for the implementation of the polymorphism in object-oriented programming languages.

Components in action

Enough of theory! Let's build a component tree based on the class hierarchy illustrated in the diagram. This way, we're going to demonstrate how we can take advantage of the composite pattern for building, user interface by using simplified syntax. We're going to take a look at a similar example in the context of Angular 2 in *Chapter 4, Getting Started with Angular 2 Components and Directives*:

```
Composite c1 = new Composite();
Composite c2 = new Composite();
Composite c3 = new Composite();

c1.components.push(c2);
c1.components.push(c3);

Leaf l1 = new Leaf();
Leaf l2 = new Leaf();
Leaf l3 = new Leaf();

c2.components.push(l1);
c2.components.push(l2);

c3.components.push(l3);
```

The preceding pseudo-code creates three instances of the Composite class and three instances of the Leaf class. The instance, c1, holds references to c2 and c3 inside the components list. The instance, c2, holds references to l1 and l2, and c3 holds reference to l3:

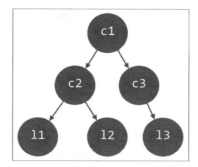

Fig. 6

The preceding diagram is a graphical representation of the component tree we built in the snippet. This is a quite simplified version of what the view in the modern JavaScript frameworks looks similar to. However, it illustrates the very basics of how we can compose directives and components. For instance, in the context of Angular 2 we can think of directives as instances of the preceding `Leaf` class (since they don't own view and thus cannot compose other directives and components), and components as instances of the `Composite` class.

If we think more abstractly for the user interface in AngularJS 1.x, we can notice that we use quite a similar approach. The templates of our views are composing different directives together in order to deliver fully a functional user interface to the end user of our application.

Components in Angular 2

Angular 2 took this approach by introducing new building blocks called **components**. Components extend the directive concept we described in the previous section, and provide broader functionality. Here is the definition of a basic `hello-world` component:

```
@Component({
  selector: 'hello-world',
  template: '<h1>Hello, {{target}}!</h1>'
})
class HelloWorld {
  target: string;
  constructor() {
    this.target = 'world';
  }
}
```

We can use it by inserting the following markup in our view:

```
<hello-world></hello-world>
```

According to the best practices, we should use an element as a selector for our components since we may have only a single component per DOM element.

The alternative ES5 syntax using the DSL Angular provides is:

```
var HelloWorld = ng.core
  .Component({
    selector: 'hello-world',
    template: '<h1>Hello, {{target}}!</h1>'
  })
  .Class({
    constructor: function () {
      this.target = 'world';
    }
  });
```

We will take a look at the preceding syntax in more detail later in the book. However, let's briefly describe the functionality, which this component provides. Once the Angular 2 application has been bootstrapped, it will look at all the elements of our DOM tree and process them. Once it finds the element called `hello-world`, it will invoke the logic associated with its definition, which means that the template of the component will be rendered and the expression between the curly brackets will be evaluated. This will result to the markup, `<h1>Hello, world!</h1>`.

So to summarize, the Angular core team separated out the directives from AngularJS 1.x into two different parts—**Components** and **Directives**. Directives provide an easy way to attach behavior to DOM elements without defining a view. Components in Angular 2 provide a powerful, and yet simple-to-learn API, which makes it easier to define the user interface of our applications. Angular 2 Components allow us to do the same amazing things as AngularJS 1.x directives, but with less typing and fewer things to learn. Components extend the Angular 2 directive concept by adding a view to it. We can think of the relation between Angular 2 components and directives the same way as the relation between `Composite` and `Leaf` from the diagram we saw in *Fig. 5*.

If we start illustrating the conceptual model of the building blocks Angular 2 provides, we can present the relation between Directive and Component as inheritance. *Chapter 4, Getting Started with Angular 2 Components and Directives* describes these two concepts in further details.

Pipes

In business applications, we often need to have different visual representations of the same piece of data. For example, if we have the number 100,000 and we want to format it as currency, most likely we won't want to display it as plain data; more likely, we'll want something like $100,000.

The responsibility for formatting data in AngularJS 1.x was assigned to filters. Another example for a data formatting requirement is when we use collections of items. For instance, if we have a list of items, we may want to filter it based on a predicate (a boolean function); in a list of numbers, we may want to display only prime numbers. AngularJS 1.x has a filter called `filter`, which allows us to do this. However, the duplication of the names often leads to confusion. That's another reason the core team renamed the filter component to **pipe**.

The motivation behind the new name is the syntax used for pipes and filters:

```
{{expression | decimal | currency}}
```

In the preceding example, we apply the pipes, `decimal` and `currency`, to the value returned by `expression`. The entire expression between the curly braces looks like Unix pipe syntax.

Defining pipes

The syntax for defining pipes is similar to the one used for the definition of directives and components. In order to create a new pipe, we can use the ES2015 decorator, `@Pipe`. It allows us to add metadata to a class, declaring it as a pipe. All we need to do is to provide a name for the pipe and define the data formatting logic. There's also an alternative ES5 syntax, which can be used if we want to skip the process of transpilation.

During runtime, once the Angular 2 expression interpreter finds out that a given expression includes a call of a pipe, it will retrieve it out of the pipes collection allocated within the component and invoke it with the appropriate arguments.

The following example illustrates how we can define a simple pipe called `lowercase1`, which transforms the given string, passed as argument to its lowercase representation:

```
@Pipe({ name: 'lowercase1' })
class LowerCasePipe1 implements PipeTransform {
  transform(value: string): string {
    if (!value) return value;
```

```
      if (typeof value !== 'string') {
        throw new Error('Invalid pipe value', value);
      }
      return value.toLowerCase();
  }
}
```

In order to be consistent, let's show the ECMAScript 5 syntax for defining pipes:

```
var LowercasePipe1 = ng.core
  .Pipe({
    name: 'lowercase'
  })
  .Class({
    constructor: function () {},
    transform: function (value) {
      if (!value) return value;
      if (typeof value === 'string') {
        throw new Error('Invalid pipe value', value);
      }
      return value.toLowerCase();
    }
  });
```

In the TypeScript syntax, we implement the `PipeTransform` interface and define the `transform` method declared inside it. However, in ECMAScript 5, we do not have support for interfaces, but we still need to implement the `transform` method in order to define a valid Angular 2 pipe. We are going to explain the TypeScript interfaces in the next chapter.

Now let's demonstrate how we can use the `lowercase1` pipe inside a component:

```
@Component({
  selector: 'app',
  pipes: [LowercasePipe1],
  template: '<h1>{{"SAMPLE" | lowercase1}}</h1>'
})
class App {}
```

And, the alternative ECMAScript 5 syntax for this is:

```
var App = ng.core.Component({
  selector: 'app',
  pipes: [LowercasePipe1],
  template: '<h1>{{"SAMPLE" | lowercase1}}</h1>'
})
```

```
.Class({
  constructor: function () {}
});
```

We can use the App component with the following markup:

```
<app></app>
```

The result we are going to see on the screen is the text sample within an h1 element.

By keeping the data formatting logic as a separate component, Angular 2 keeps the strong separation of concerns that can be seen throughout. We will take a look at how we can define stateful and stateless pipes for our application in *Chapter 7, Building a real-life application while exploring pipes and http.*

Change detection

As we saw earlier, the view in MVC updates itself, based on change events it receives from the model. A number of **Model View Whatever (MVW)** frameworks took this approach, and embedded the observer pattern in the core of their change detection mechanism.

Classical change detection

Let's take a look at a simple example, which doesn't use any framework. Suppose we have a model called User, which has a property called name:

```
class User extends EventEmitter {
  private name: string;
  setName(name: string) {
    this.name = name;
    this.emit('change');
  }
  getName(): string {
    return this.name;
  }
}
```

The preceding snippet uses TypeScript. Do not worry if the syntax does not look familiar to you, we're going to make an introduction to the language in the next chapter.

The user class extends the class, EventEmitter. This provides primitives for emitting and subscribing to events.

Now let's define a view, which displays the name of an instance of the User class, passed as an argument to its constructor:

```
class View {
  constructor(user: User, el: Element /* a DOM element */) {
    el.innerHTML = user.getName();
  }
}
```

We can initialize the view element by:

```
let user = new User();
user.setName('foo');
let view = new View(user, document.getElementById('label'));
```

As the end result, the user will see a label with the content, foo. However, changes in user will not be reflected by the view. In order to update the view when the name of the user changes, we need to subscribe to the change event and then update the content of the DOM element. We need to update the View definition in the following way:

```
class View {
  constructor(user: User, el: any /* a DOM element */) {
    el.innerHTML = user.getName();
    user.on('change', () => {
      el.innerHTML = user.getName();
    });
  }
}
```

This is how most frameworks used to implement their change detection before the era of AngularJS 1.x.

AngularJS 1.x change detection

Most beginners are fascinated by the data-binding mechanism in AngularJS 1.x. The basic Hello World example looks similar to this:

```
function MainCtrl($scope) {
  $scope.label = 'Hello world!';
}

<body ng-app ng-controller="MainCtrl">
  {{label}}
</body>
```

If you run this, Hello world! magically appears onto the screen. However, that is not even the most impressive thing! If we add a text input and we bind it to the label property of the scope, each change will reflect the content displayed by the interpolation directive:

```
<body ng-controller="MainCtrl">
  <input ng-model="label">
  {{label}}
</body>
```

How awesome is that! This is one of the main selling points of AngularJS 1.x—the extreme ease of achieving data-binding. We add two (four if we count ng-controller and ng-app) attributes in our markup, add property to a mystical object called $scope, which is magically passed to a custom function we define, and everything simply works!

However, the more experienced Angular developer has a better understanding of what is actually going on behind the scene. In the preceding example, inside the directives, ng-model and ng-bind (in our case, the interpolation directive, {{}}), Angular adds watchers with different behavior associated to the same expression—label. These watchers are quite similar to the observers in the classical MVC pattern. On some specific events (in our case, change of the content of the text input), AngularJS will loop over all such watchers, evaluate the expressions associated to them in the context of a given scope, and store their results. This loop is known as the digest loop.

In the preceding examples, the evaluation of the expression, label, in the context of the scope will return the text, Hello world!. On each iteration, AngularJS will compare the current result of the evaluation with the previous result, and will invoke the associated callback in case the values differ. For instance, the callback added by the interpolation directive will set the content of the element to be the new result of the expression's evaluation. This is an example of the dependency between the callbacks of the watchers of two directives. The callback of the watcher added by ng-model modifies the result of the expression associated to the watcher added by the interpolation directive.

However, this approach has its own drawbacks. We said that the digest loop will be invoked on some specific events, but what if these events happen outside the framework, for example? What if we use setTimeout and inside the callback, passed as the first argument, we change properties attached to the scope that we're watching? AngularJS will be unaware of the change and won't invoke the digest loop, so we need to do that explicitly using $scope.$apply. But what if the framework knew about all the asynchronous events happening in the browser, such as user events, XMLHttpRequest events, WebSockets related events, and others? In such a case, AngularJS would be able to intercept the event's handling and could invoke the digest loop without forcing us to do so!

In the zone.js

That's exactly the case in Angular 2. This functionality is implemented with zones using `zone.js`.

At ng-conf in 2014, Brian Ford gave a talk about zones. Brian presented zones as meta-monkey patching of browser APIs. Recently Miško Hevery proposed to TC39 more mature zones API for standardization. `Zone.js` is a library developed by the Angular team, which implements zones in JavaScript. They represent an execution context, which allow us to intercept asynchronous browser calls. Basically, by using zones, we are able to invoke a piece of logic just after the given `XMLHttpRequest` completes or when we receive a new `WebSocket` event. Angular 2 took advantage of `zone.js` by intercepting asynchronous browser events and invoking the `digest` loop just at the right time. This totally eliminates the need of explicit calls of the `digest` loop by the developer using Angular.

Simplified data flow

The cross-watcher dependencies may create a tangled data flow in our application, which is hard to follow. This may lead to unpredictable behavior and bugs, which are hard to find. Although Angular 2 kept the dirty checking as a way for achieving change detection, it enforced unidirectional data flow. This happened by disallowing dependencies between the different watchers, which allows the `digest` loop to be run only once. This strategy increases the performance of our applications dramatically, and reduces the complexity of the data flow. Angular 2 also made improvements to memory efficiency and the performance of the `digest` loop. Further details on Angular 2's change detection and the different strategies used for its implementation can be found in *Chapter 4, Getting Started with Angular 2 Components and Directives*.

Enhancing AngularJS 1.x's change detection

Now let's take a step back and again think about the change detection mechanism of the framework.

We said that inside the `digest` loop, Angular evaluates registered expressions and compares the evaluated values with the values associated with the same expressions in the previous iteration of the loop.

The most optimal algorithm used for the comparison may differ depending on the type of the value returned from the expression's evaluation. For instance, if we get a mutable list of items, we need to loop over the entire collection and compare the items in the collections one by one in order to verify that there is a change or not. However, if we have an immutable list, we can perform a check with a constant complexity, only by comparing references. This is the case because the instances of immutable data structures cannot change. Instead of applying an operation, which intends to modify such instances, we'll get a new reference with the modification applied.

In AngularJS 1.x, we can add watchers using a few methods. Two of them are `$watch(exp, fn, deep)` or `$watchCollection(exp, fn)`. These methods give us some level of control over the way the change detection will perform the equality check. For example, adding a watcher by using `$watch` and passing a `false` value as a third argument will make AngularJS perform a reference check (that is compare the current value with the previous one using `===`). However, if we pass a truthy (any `true` value), the check will be deep (that is using `angular.equals`). This way, depending on the expected type of the returned by the expression value, we can add listeners in the most appropriate way in order to allow the framework to perform equality checks with the most optimal algorithm available. This API has two limitations:

- It does not allow you to choose the most appropriate equality check algorithm at runtime.
- It does not allow you to extend the change detection to third-parties for their specific data structures.

The Angular core team assigned this responsibility to differs, allowing them to extend the change detection mechanism and optimize it, based on the data we use in our applications. Angular 2 defines two base classes, which we can extend in order to define custom algorithms:

- `KeyValueDiffer`: This allows us to perform advanced diffing over key-value-based data structures.
- `IterableDiffer`: This allows us to perform advanced diffing over list-like data structures.

Angular 2 allows us to take full control over the change detection mechanism by extending it with custom algorithms, which wasn't possible in the previous version of the framework. We'll take a further look into the change detection and how we can configure it in *Chapter 4, Getting Started with Angular 2 Components and Directives*.

Understanding services

Services are the building blocks that Angular provides for the definition of the business logic of our applications. In AngularJS 1.x, we had three different ways for defining services:

```
// The Factory method
module.factory('ServiceName', function (dep1, dep2, …) {
  return {
    // public API
  };
});

// The Service method
module.service('ServiceName', function (dep1, dep2, …) {
  // public API
  this.publicProp = val;
});

// The Provider method
module.provider('ServiceName', function () {
  return {
    $get: function (dep1, dep2, …) {
      return {
        // public API
      };
    }
  };
});
```

Although the first two syntactical variations provide similar functionality, they differ in the way the registered directive will be instantiated. The third syntax allows further configuration of the registered provider during configuration time.

Having three different methods for defining services is quite confusing for the AngularJS 1.x beginners. Let's think for a second what necessitated the introduction of these methods for registering services. Why can't we simply use JavaScript constructor functions, object literals, or ES2015 classes instead, which Angular will not be aware of? We could encapsulate our business logic inside a custom JavaScript constructor function like this:

```
function UserTransactions(id) {
  this.userId = id;
}
UserTransactions.prototype.makeTransaction = function (amount) {
```

```
    // method logic
  };

  module.controller('MainCtrl', function () {
    this.submitClick = function () {
      new UserTransactions(this.userId).makeTransaction(this.amount);
    };
  });
```

This code is completely valid. However, it doesn't take advantage of one of the key features that AngularJS 1.x provides—the DI mechanism. The `MainCtrl` function uses the constructor function, `UserTransaction`, which is visible in its body. The preceding code has two main pitfalls:

- We're coupled with the logic used for the service's instantiation.
- The code is not testable. In order to mock `UserTransactions`, we need to monkey patch it.

How does AngularJS deal with these two things? When a given service is required, through the DI mechanism of the framework, AngularJS resolves all of its dependencies and instantiates it by passing them to the `factory` function, which encapsulates the logic for its creation. The `factory` function is passed as the second argument to the `factory` and `service` methods. The `provider` method allows definition of a service on lower level; the `factory` method there is the one under the `$get` property of the provider.

Just like AngularJS 1.x, Angular 2 tolerates this separation of concerns as well, so the core team kept the services. In contrast to AngularJS 1.x, the last major version of the framework provides a much simpler interface for the definition of services by allowing us to use plain ES2015 classes or ES5 constructor functions. We cannot escape from the fact that we need to explicitly state which services should be available for injection and somehow specify instructions for their instantiation. However, Angular 2 uses the ES2016 decorator's syntax for this purpose instead of the methods familiar to us from AngularJS 1.x. This allows us to define the services in our applications as simple as ES2015 classes, with decorators for configuration of the DI:

```
  import {Inject, Injectable} from '@angular/core';

  @Injectable()
  class HttpService {
    constructor() { /* … */ }
  }

  @Injectable()
  class User {
```

```
    constructor(private service: HttpService) {}
    save() {
      return this.service.post('/users')
        .then(res => {
          this.id = res.id;
          return this;
        });
    }
  }
}
```

The alternative ECMAScript 5 syntax is:

```
var HttpService = ng.core.Class({
  constructor: function () {}
});
var User = ng.core.Class({
  constructor: [HttpService, function (service) {
    this.service = service;
  }],
  save: function () {
    return this.service.post('/users')
      .then(function (res) {
        this.id = res.id;
        return this;
      });
  }
});
```

Services are related to the components and the directives described in the previous sections. For developing highly coherent and reusable UI components, we need to move all the business-related logic to inside our services. And, in order to develop testable components, we need to take advantage of the DI mechanism for resolving all their dependencies.

A core difference between the services in Angular 2 and AngularJS 1.x is the way their dependencies are being resolved and represented internally. AngularJS 1.x is using strings for identifying the different services and the associated factories used for their instantiation. However, Angular 2 uses keys instead. Usually the keys are the types of the distinct services. Another core difference in the instantiation is the hierarchical structure of injectors, which encapsulate different dependency providers with different visibility.

Another distinction between the services in the last two major versions of the framework is the simplified syntax. Although Angular 2 uses ES2015 classes for the definition of our business logic, you can use ECMAScript 5 `constructor` functions as well or use the DSL provided by the framework. The DI in Angular 2 has a completely different syntax and has improved behavior by providing a consistent way of injecting dependencies. The syntax used in the preceding example uses ES2016 decorators, and in *Chapter 5, Dependency Injection in Angular 2*, we'll take a look at alternative syntax, which uses ECMAScript 5. You can also find more detailed explanation of Angular 2 services and DI in *Chapter 5, Dependency Injection in Angular 2*.

Understanding the new component-based router

In traditional web applications, all the page changes are associated with a full-page reload, which fetches all of the referenced resources and data and renders the entire page onto the screen. However, requirements for web applications have evolved over time.

Single-page applications (SPAs) that we build with Angular simulate desktop user experiences. This often involve incremental loading of the resources and data required by the application, and no full-page reloads after the initial page load. Often the different pages or views in SPAs are represented by different templates, which are loaded asynchronously and rendered on a specific position on the screen. Later, when the template with all the required resources is loaded and the route is changed, the logic attached to the selected page is invoked and populates the template with data. If the user presses the refresh button after the given page in our SPA is loaded, the same page needs to be re-rendered after the refresh of the view completes. This involves similar behavior—finding the requested view, fetching the required template with all referenced resources, and invoking the logic associated with that view.

What template needs to be fetched, and the logic which should be invoked after the page reloads successfully, depends on the selected view before the user pressed the refresh button. The framework determines this by parsing the page URL, which contains the identifier of the currently selected page, represented in the hierarchical structure.

All the responsibilities related to the navigation, changing the URL, loading the appropriate template, and invoking specific logic when the view is loaded are assigned to the router component. These are some quite challenging tasks, and support for different navigation APIs required for cross-browser compatibility makes the implementation of routing in modern SPAs a non-trivial problem.

AngularJS 1.x introduced the router in its core, which was later externalized into the ngRoute component. It allows a declarative way for defining the different views in our SPA, by providing a template for each page and a piece of logic that needs to be invoked when a page is selected. However, the functionality of the router is limited. It does not support essential features such as nested view routing. That's one of the reasons most developers preferred to use ui-router, developed by the community. Both AngularJS 1.x's router, and ui-router, route-definitions include a route configuration object, which defines a template and a controller associated with the page.

As described in the previous sections, Angular 2 changed the building blocks it provides for the development of SPAs. Angular 2 removes the floating controllers, and instead represents views as a composition of components. This necessitates the development of a brand new router, which empowers these new concepts.

The core differences between the AngularJS 1.x router and the Angular 2 router are:

- The Angular 2 router is component based, ngRoute is not.
- There is now support for nested views.
- Different syntax empowered by ES2016 decorators.

Angular 2 route definition syntax

Let's take a brief look at the new syntax used by the Angular 2 router to define routes in our applications:

```
import {Component} from '@angular/core';
import {bootstrap} from '@angular/platform-browser-dynamic';
import {RouteConfig, ROUTER_DIRECTIVES,
ROUTER_PROVIDERS} from '@angular/router-deprecated';

import {Home} from './components/home/home';
import {About} from './components/about/about';

@Component({
  selector: 'app',
  templateUrl: './app.html',
  directives: [ROUTER_DIRECTIVES]
})
@RouteConfig([
  { path: '/', component: Home, name: 'home' },
  { path: '/about', component: About, name: 'about' }
])
class App {}

bootstrap(App, [ROUTER_PROVIDERS]);
```

We won't go into too much detail here since *Chapter 6, Angular 2 forms and the new component-based router* and *Chapter 7, Building a real-life application while exploring pipes and http,* are dedicated to the new router, but let's mention the main points in the preceding code snippet.

The router lives in the module, @angular/router-deprecated. There, we can find the directives it defines, the decorator used for the configuration of the routes and ROUTER_PROVIDERS.

 We'll take a further look at ROUTER_PROVIDERS in *Chapter 7, Building a real-life application while exploring pipes and http.*

The parameter passed to the @RouteConfig decorator shows how we define the routes in our application. We use an array with objects, which defines the mappings between routes and the components associated with them. Inside the Component decorator, we explicitly state that we want to use the directives contained within ROUTER_DIRECTIVES, which are related to the router's usage inside the templates.

Summary

In this chapter, we took a quick overview of the main building blocks for developing SPAs provided by Angular 2. We pointed out the core differences between these components in AngularJS 1.x and Angular 2.

Although we can use ES2015, or even ES5, for building Angular 2 applications, the recommendation from Google is to take advantage of the language used for the development of the framework—TypeScript.

In the next chapter, we'll take a look at TypeScript and how we can start using it in your next application. We will also explain how we can take advantage of the static typing in the JavaScript libraries and frameworks written in vanilla JavaScript, with ambient type annotations.

TypeScript Crash Course

3

In this chapter, we are going to start working with TypeScript, the language Angular 2 recommends for scripting. All the features ECMAScript 2015 and respectively ECMAScript 2016 provides, such as functions, classes, modules, and decorators, are already implemented in or added to the roadmap of TypeScript. Because of the extra type annotations, there are some syntactical additions compared to JavaScript.

For smoother transition from the language we already know - ES5, we will start with some common features between ES2016 and TypeScript. Where there are differences between the ES syntax and TypeScript, we'll explicitly mention it. In the second half of the chapter, we'll add the type annotations to everything we've learned until this point.

Later in the chapter, we will explain the extra features TypeScript provides, such as static typing and extended syntax. We will discuss the different consequences based on these features, which will help us be more productive and less error-prone. Let's get going!

Introduction to TypeScript

TypeScript is an open source programming language that is developed and maintained by Microsoft. Its initial public release was in October 2012. TypeScript is a superset of ECMAScript, supporting all of the syntax and semantics of JavaScript with some extra features on top, such as static typing and richer syntax.

Fig. 1 shows the relationship between ES5, ES2015, ES2016, and TypeScript.

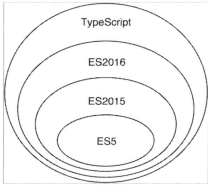

Fig. 1

Because TypeScript is statically typed, it can provide a number of benefits to us as JavaScript developers. Let's have a quick look at those benefits now.

Compile-time type checking

Some of the most common mistakes we make while writing JavaScript code is to misspell a property or a method name. We'll find out about the mistake when we get a runtime error. This can happen during development as well as in production. Hoping we will know about the error before we deploy our code to production environment isn't a comfortable feeling! However, this is not a problem specific to JavaScript; it is something common to all the dynamic languages. Even with lots of unit tests, these errors can slip by.

TypeScript provides a compiler, which takes care of such mistakes for us by using static code analysis. If we take advantage of static typing, TypeScript will be aware of the existing properties a given object has, and if we misspell any of them, the compiler will warn us with a compile-time error.

Another great benefit of TypeScript is that it allows large teams to collaborate, since it provides formal, verifiable naming. This way, it allows us to write easy-to-understand code.

Better support by text editors and IDEs

There are a number of tools, such as **Tern** or **Google Closure Compiler**, that are trying to bring better autocompletion support for JavaScript in text editors and IDEs. However, as JavaScript is a dynamic language, it is impossible for the IDEs and text editors to make sophisticated suggestions without any metadata.

Annotating the code with such metadata is a built-in feature of TypeScript known as type annotations. Based on them, text editors and IDEs can perform better static analysis over our code. This provides better refactoring tools and autocompletion, which increases our productivity and allows us to make fewer mistakes while writing the source code for our applications.

There's even more to TypeScript

TypeScript by itself has a number of other benefits:

- **It is a superset of JavaScript**: All JavaScript (ES5 and ES2015) programs are already valid TypeScript ones. In essence, you have already been writing TypeScript code. Since it is based on the latest version of the ECMAScript standard, it allows us to take advantage of the latest bleeding edge syntax provided by the language.

- **Supports optional type checking**: If, for any reason, we decide that we don't want to explicitly define the type of a variable or a method, we can just skip the type definition. However, we should be aware that this means we are no longer taking advantage of the static typing, so we are giving up on all the benefits mentioned earlier.

- **Developed and maintained by Microsoft**: The quality of the implementation of the language is very high and it is unlikely that support will be dropped unexpectedly. TypeScript is based on the work of some of the world's best experts in programming language development.

- **It is open source**: This allows the community to freely contribute to the language and suggest features, which are discussed in an open manner. The fact that TypeScript is open source allows for the easier development of third-party extensions and tools, which extends further the scope of its usage.

Since modern browsers do not support TypeScript natively, there is a compiler that translates the TypeScript code we write into readable JavaScript in a predefined target version of ECMAScript. Once the code is compiled, all the type annotations are removed.

Using TypeScript

Let's start writing some TypeScript!

In the following sections, we are going to take a look at different snippets showing some of the features of TypeScript. In order to be able to run the snippets and play with them yourself, you'll need to install the TypeScript compiler on your computer. Let's take a look at how to do this.

TypeScript is best installed using **Node Package Manager (npm)**. I'd recommend you to use npm Version 3.0.0 or newer. If you don't have node.js and npm installed already, you can visit https://nodejs.org and follow the instructions there.

Installing TypeScript with npm

Once you have npm installed and running, verify that you have the latest version by opening your terminal window and running the following command:

```
$ npm -v
```

In order to install TypeScript 1.8, use:

```
$ npm install -g typescript@1.8
```

The preceding command will install the TypeScript compiler and add its executable (tsc) as global to your path.

In order to verify that everything works properly, you can use:

```
$ tsc -v
Version 1.8.0
```

The output should be similar to the preceding one, though possibly with a different version.

Running our first TypeScript program

 You can find the code for this book on the following URL: https://github.com/mgechev/switching-to-angular2. As a comment in most code snippets you'll find a relative to the app directory file path where you can find them.

Now, let's compile our first TypeScript program! Create a file called `hello.ts` and enter the following content:

```
// ch3/hello-world/hello-world.ts
console.log('Hello world!');
```

Since you've already installed the TypeScript compiler, you should have a global executable command called `tsc`. You can use it in order to compile the file:

```
$ tsc hello.ts
```

Now, you should see the file `hello.js` in the same directory where `hello.ts` is. `hello.js` is the output of the TypeScript compiler; it contains the JavaScript equivalent to the TypeScript you wrote. You can run this file using the following command:

```
$ node hello.js
```

Now, you'll see the string `Hello world!` printed on the screen. In order to combine the process of compiling and running the program, you can use the package `ts-node`:

```
$ npm install -g ts-node
```

Now you can run:

```
$ ts-node hello.ts
```

You should see the same result, but without the `ts-node` file stored on the disk.

TypeScript syntax and features introduced by ES2015 and ES2016

As TypeScript is a superset of JavaScript, before we start learning about its syntax, it's a little easier to start by introducing some of the bigger changes in ES2015 and ES2016; to understand TypeScript, we first must understand ES2015 and ES2016. We're going to have a whistle-stop tour through these changes before diving in to TypeScript proper later.

A detailed explanation of ES2015 and ES2016 is outside the scope of this book. In order to get familiar with all the new features and syntaxes, I strongly recommend you to take a look at *Exploring ES6: upgrade to the next version of JavaScript* by *Dr. Axel Rauschmayer*.

The next couple of pages will introduce new standards and allow you to take advantage of most of the features you're going to need in the development of Angular 2 applications.

ES2015 arrow functions

JavaScript has first class functions, which means that they can be passed around like any other value:

```
// ch3/arrow-functions/simple-reduce.ts
var result = [1, 2, 3].reduce(function (total, current) {
  return total + current;
}, 0); // 6
```

This syntax is great; however, it is a bit too verbose. ES2015 introduced a new syntax to define anonymous functions called the arrow function syntax. Using it, we can create anonymous functions, as seen in the following examples:

```
// ch3/arrow-functions/arrow-functions.ts

// example 1
var result = [1, 2, 3]
  .reduce((total, current) => total + current, 0);

console.log(result);


// example 2
var even = [3, 1, 56, 7].filter(el => !(el % 2));

console.log(even);


// example 3
var sorted = data.sort((a, b) => {
  var diff = a.price - b.price;
  if (diff !== 0) {
    return diff;
  }
  return a.total - b.total;
});
```

In the first example, we got the total sum of the elements in the array [1, 2, 3]. In the second example, we got all the even numbers inside the array [3, 1, 56, 7]. In the third example, we sorted an array by the properties' price and total in the ascending order.

Arrow functions have a few more features that we need to look at. The most important one of them is that they keep the context (`this`) from the surrounding code:

```
// ch3/arrow-functions/context-demo.ts
function MyComponent() {
  this.age = 42;
  setTimeout(() => {
    this.age += 1;
    console.log(this.age);
  }, 100);
}
new MyComponent(); // 43 in 100ms.
```

For example, when we invoke the function `MyComponent` with the operator `new`, this will point to the new object instantiated by the call. The arrow function will keep the context (`this`), in the callback of `setTimeout`, and print **43** on the screen.

This is extremely useful in Angular 2, since the binding context for a given component is its instance (that is, its `this`). If we define `MyComponent` as an Angular 2 component and we have a binding to the `age` property, the preceding code will be valid and all the bindings will work (notice that we don't have scope, neither do we have explicit calls to the `$digest` loop although we have called `setTimeout` directly).

Using the ES2015 and ES2016 classes

When developers new to JavaScript hear that the language empowers the **object-oriented (OO)** paradigm, they're normally confused when they discover that there's no syntax for the definition of classes. This perception was born by the fact that some of the most popular programming languages, such as Java, C#, and C++, have the concept of classes used for the construction of objects. However, JavaScript implements the OO paradigm differently. JavaScript has a prototype-based, object-oriented programming model, where we can instantiate objects using the object literal syntax or functions (also known as the constructor functions) and we can take advantage of the inheritance using the so-called prototype chain.

Though this is a valid way to implement the OO paradigm and the semantics are similar to the one in the classical object-oriented model, it is confusing for inexperienced JavaScript developers who are not sure how to process this properly. This is one of the reasons TC39 decided to provide an alternative syntax to exploit the object-oriented paradigm in the language. Behind the scenes, the new syntax has the same semantics as the one we're used to, like using the constructor functions and the prototype-based inheritance. However, it provides a more convenient syntax to empower the OO paradigm's features with less boilerplate.

ES2016 adds some extra syntax to the ES2015 classes, such as static and instance property declaration.

Here is an example that demonstrates the syntax used to define the classes in ES2016:

```
// ch3/es6-classes/sample-classes.ts

class Human {
  static totalPeople = 0;
  _name; // ES2016 property declaration syntax
  constructor(name) {
    this._name = name;
    Human.totalPeople += 1;
  }
  get name() {
    return this._name;
  }
  set name(val) {
    this._name = val;
  }
  talk() {
    return `Hi, I'm ${this.name}!`;
  }
}

class Developer extends Human {
  _languages; // ES2016 property declaration syntax
  constructor(name, languages) {
    super(name);
    this._languages = languages;
  }
  get languages() {
    return this._languages;
  }
  talk() {
    return `${super.talk()} And I know
${this.languages.join(',')}.`;
  }
}
```

In ES2015, the explicit declaration of the _name property is not required; however, since the TypeScript compiler should be aware during compile-time of the existing properties of the instances of a given class, we would need to add the declaration of the property to the class declaration itself.

The preceding snippet is both a valid TypeScript and JavaScript code. In it, we defined a class called Human, which adds a single property to the objects instantiated by it. It does this by setting its value to the parameter name passed to its constructor.

Now, open the ch3/es6-classes/sample-classes.ts file and play around with it! You can create different instances of the classes the same way you create objects using constructor functions:

```
var human = new Human("foobar");
var dev = new Developer("bar", ["JavaScript"]);
console.log(dev.talk());
```

In order to execute the code, run the following command:

```
$ ts-node sample-classes.ts
```

Classes are commonly used in Angular 2. You can use them to define your components, directives, services, and pipes. However, you can also use the alternative ES5 syntax, which takes advantage of the constructor functions. Under the hood, once the TypeScript code is compiled, there would be no such significant difference between both the syntaxes, because the ES2015 classes are being transpiled to constructor functions anyway.

Defining variables with block scope

Another confusing point of JavaScript for developers with a different background is the variable scope in the language. In Java and C++, for example, we're used to the block lexical scope. This means that a given variable defined inside a specific block will be visible only inside that block and all of the nested blocks inside of it.

However, in JavaScript, things are a little bit different. ECMAScript defines a functional lexical scope that has similar semantics to the block lexical scope, but it uses functions instead of blocks. This means that we have the following:

```
// ch3/let/var.ts

var fns = [];
for (var i = 0; i < 5; i += 1) {
  fns.push(function() {
    console.log(i);
  })
}
fns.forEach(fn => fn());
```

This has some weird implications. Once the code has been executed, it will log five times the number 5.

ES2015 added a new syntax to define the variables with block-scope visibility. The syntax is similar to the current one. However, instead of var, it uses the keyword let:

```
// ch3/let/let.ts

var fns = [];
for (let i = 0; i < 5; i += 1) {
  fns.push(function() {
    console.log(i);
  })
}
fns.forEach(fn => fn());
```

Meta-programming with ES2016 decorators

JavaScript is a dynamic language that allows us to easily modify and/or alter the behavior to suit the programs we write. Decorators are a proposal to ES2016, which according to the design document https://github.com/wycats/javascript-decorators:

> "...*make it possible to annotate and modify classes and properties at design time.*"

Their syntaxes are quite similar to the annotations in Java, and they are even closer to the decorators in Python. ES2016 decorators are used commonly in Angular 2 to define components, directives, and pipes, and to take advantage of the dependency injection mechanism of the framework. Essentially, most use cases of decorators involve altering the behavior to predefined logic or adding some metadata to different constructs.

ES2016 decorators allow us to do a lot of fancy things by changing the behavior of our programs. Typical use cases could be to annotate the given methods or properties as deprecated or read-only. A set of predefined decorators that can improve the readability of the code we produce can be found in a project by *Jay Phelps* called *core-decorators.js*. Another use case is taking advantage of the proxy-based aspect-oriented programming using a declarative syntax. The library providing this functionality is aspect.js.

In general, ES2016 decorators are just another syntax sugar, which translates to the code we're already familiar with from the previous versions of JavaScript. Let's take a look at a simple example from the proposal's draft:

```
// ch3/decorators/nonenumerable.ts

class Person {
```

```
  @nonenumerable
  get kidCount() {
    return 42;
  }
}

function nonenumerable(target, name, descriptor) {
  descriptor.enumerable = false;
  return descriptor;
}

var person = new Person();

for (let prop in person) {
  console.log(prop);
}
```

In this case, we have an ES2015 class called `Person` with a single getter called `kidCount`. Over the `kidCount` getter, we have applied the `nonenumerable` decorator. The decorator is a function that accepts a target (the `Person` class), the name of the target property we intend to decorate (`kidCount`), and the descriptor of the `target` property. After we change the descriptor, we need to return it in order to apply the modification. Basically, the decorator's application could be translated into ECMAScript 5 in the following way:

```
descriptor = nonenumerable (Person.prototype, 'kidCount', descriptor)
|| descriptor;
Object.defineProperty(Person.prototype, 'kidCount', descriptor);
```

Using configurable decorators

Here is an example on using the decorators defined by Angular 2:

```
@Component({
  selector: 'app',
  providers: [NamesList],
  templateUrl: './app.html',
  directives: [RouterOutlet, RouterLink]
})
@RouteConfig([
  { path: '/', component: Home, name: 'home' },
  { path: '/about', component: About, name: 'about' }
])
export class App {}
```

When decorators accept arguments (just like `Component`, `RouteConfig`, and `View` in the preceding example), they need to be defined as functions that accept arguments and return the actual decorator:

```
function Component(config) {
  // validate properties
  return (componentCtrl) => {
    // apply decorator
  };
}
```

In this example, we defined a configurable decorator called `Component` that accepts a single argument called `config` and returns a decorator.

Writing modular code with ES2015

Another problem that JavaScript professionals have experienced along the years is the lack of a module system in the language. Initially, the community developed different patterns, aiming to enforce the modularity and the encapsulation of the software we produce. Such patterns included the module pattern, which takes advantage of the functional lexical scope and closures. Another example is the namespace pattern, which represents the different namespaces as nested objects. AngularJS 1.x introduced its own module system that unfortunately doesn't provide features like lazy module loading. However, these patterns were more like workarounds rather than real solutions.

CommonJS (used in node.js) and **AMD (Asynchronous Module Definition)** were later invented. They are still in wide use today and provide features, such as handling of circular dependencies, asynchronous module loading (in AMD), and so on.

TC39 took the best of the existing module systems and introduced this concept on a language level. ES2015 provides two APIs to define and consume modules. They are as follows:

- Declarative API.
- Imperative API using the module loader.

Angular 2 takes full advantage of the ES2015 module system, so let's dive into it! In this section, we are going to take a look at the syntax used for the declarative definition and consumption of modules. We are also going to peek at the module loader's API in order to see how we can programmatically load modules in an explicit asynchronous manner.

Using the ES2015 module syntax

Let's take a look at an example:

```
// ch3/modules/math.ts

export function square(x) {
  return Math.pow(x, 2);
};
export function log10(x) {
  return Math.log10(x);
};
export const PI = Math.PI;
```

In the preceding snippet, we defined a simple ES2015 module in the file `math.ts`. We can think of it as a sample math Angular 2 utility module. Inside it, we defined and exported the functions `square` and `log10`, and the constant `PI`. The `const` keyword is another keyword brought by ES2015 that is used to define constants. As you can see, what we do is nothing more than prefixing the function's definitions with the keyword `export`. If we want to export the entire functionality in the end and skip the duplicate explicit usage of `export`, we can:

```
// ch3/modules/math2.ts

function square(x) {
  return Math.pow(x, 2);
};
function log10(x) {
  return Math.log10(x);
};
const PI = Math.PI;
export { square, log10, PI };
```

The syntax on the last line is nothing more than an enhanced object literal syntax, introduced by ES2015. Now, let's take a look at how we can consume this module:

```
// ch3/modules/app.ts

import {square, log10} from './math';
console.log(square(2)); // 4
console.log(log10(10)); // 1
```

As an identifier of the module, we used its relative path to the current file. By using destructuring, we imported the required functions—in this case, `square` and `log10`.

Taking advantage of the implicit asynchronous behavior

It is important to note that the ES2015 module syntax has implicit asynchronous behavior.

Let's say we have modules A, B, and C. Module A uses modules B and C, so it depends on them. Once the user requires module A, the JavaScript module loader would need to load modules B and C before being able to invoke any of the logic that resides in module A because of the dependencies we have. However, modules B and C will be loaded asynchronously. Once they are loaded completely, the JavaScript virtual machine will be able to execute module A.

Using aliases

Another typical situation is when we want to use an alias for a given export. For example, if we use a third-party library, we may want to rename any of its exports in order to escape name collisions or just to have a more convenient naming:

```
import {bootstrap as initialize} from '@angular/platform-browser-
dynamic';
```

Importing all the module exports

We can import the entire `math` module using:

```
// ch3/modules/app2.ts

import * as math from './math';
console.log(math.square(2)); // 4
console.log(math.log10(10)); // 1
console.log(math.PI); // 3.141592653589793
```

The semantics behind this syntax is quite similar to CommonJS, although in the browser, we have implicit asynchronous behavior.

Default exports

If a given module defines an export, which would quite likely be used by any of its consumer modules, we can take advantage of the default export syntax:

```
// ch3/modules/math3.ts

export default function cube(x) {
  return Math.pow(x, 3);
```

```
};
export function square(x) {
  return Math.pow(x, 2);
};
```

In order to consume this module, we can use the following `app.ts` file:

```
// ch3/modules/app3.ts

import cube from './math3';
console.log(cube(3)); // 27
```

Or, if we want to import the default export as well as some other exports, we can use:

```
// ch3/modules/app4.ts

import cube, { square } from './math3';
console.log(square(2)); // 4
console.log(cube(3)); // 27
```

In general, the default export is nothing more than a named export named with the reserved word `default`:

```
// ch3/modules/app5.ts

import { default as cube } from './math3';
console.log(cube(3)); // 27
```

ES2015 module loader

The new version of the standard defines a programmatic API to work with modules. This is the so-called module loader API. It allows us to define and import modules, or configure the module loading.

Let's suppose we have the following module definition in the file `app.js`:

```
import { square } from './math';
export function main() {
  console.log(square(2)); // 4
}
```

From the file `init.js`, we can programmatically load the `app` module and invoke its `main` function using:

```
System.import('./app')
  .then(app => {
    app.main();
```

```
  })
  .catch(error => {
    console.log('Terrible error happened', error);
  });
```

The global object System has a method called import that allows us to import modules using their identifier. In the preceding snippet, we imported the module app defined in app.js. System.import returns a promise that could be resolved on success or rejected in case of an error. Once the promise is resolved as the first parameter of the callback passed to then, we will get the module itself. The first parameter of the callback registered in case of rejection is the error that happened.

The code from the last snippet does not exist in the GitHub repository, since it requires some additional configuration. We are going to apply the module loader more explicitly in the Angular 2 examples in the next chapters of the book.

ES2015 and ES2016 recap

Congratulations! We're more than halfway toward learning TypeScript. All the features we've just seen are a part of TypeScript, since it implements a superset of JavaScript and since all these features are an upgrade on top of the current syntax, they are easy to grasp by experienced JavaScript developers.

In the next sections, we will describe all the amazing features of TypeScript that are outside the intersection with ECMAScript.

Taking advantage of static typing

Static typing is what can provide better tooling for our development process. While writing JavaScript, the most that IDEs and text editors can do is syntax highlighting and providing some basic autocompletion suggestions based on the sophisticated static analysis of our code. This means that we can only verify that we haven't made any typos by running the code.

In the previous sections, we described only the new features provided by ECMAScript expected to be implemented by browsers in the near future. In this section, we will take a look at what TypeScript provides in order to help us be less error-prone and more productive. At the time of this writing, there're no plans to implement built-in support for static typing in the browsers.

The TypeScript code goes through intermediate preprocessing that performs the type checking and drops all the type annotations in order to provide valid JavaScript supported by modern browsers.

Using explicit type definitions

Just like Java and C++, TypeScript allows us to explicitly declare the type of the given variable:

```
let foo: number = 42;
```

The preceding line defines the variable `foo` in the current block using the `let` syntax. We explicitly declare that we want `foo` to be of the type `number` and we set the value of `foo` to 42.

Now let's try to change the value of `foo`:

```
let foo: number = 42;
foo = '42';
```

Here, after the declaration of `foo`, we will set its value to the string `'42'`. This is a perfectly valid JavaScript code; however, if we compile it using the TypeScript's compiler, we will get:

```
$ tsc basic.ts
basic.ts(2,1): error TS2322: Type 'string' is not assignable to
    type 'number'.
```

Once `foo` has been associated with the given type, we cannot assign it values belonging to different types. This is one of the reasons we can skip the explicit type definition in case we assign a value to the given variable:

```
let foo = 42;
foo = '42';
```

The semantics behind this code will be the same as the one with the explicit type definition because of the type inference of TypeScript. We'll further take a look at it at the end of this chapter.

The type any

All the types in TypeScript are subtypes of a type called `any`. We can declare variables belonging to the `any` type by using the `any` keyword. Such variables can hold the value of `any` type:

```
let foo: any;
foo = {};
foo = 'bar ';
foo += 42;
console.log(foo); // "bar 42"
```

The preceding code is a valid TypeScript, and it will not throw any error during compilation or runtime. If we use the type `any` for all of our variables, we will be basically writing the code with dynamic typing, which drops all the benefits of the TypeScript's compiler. That's why we have to be careful with `any` and use it only when it is necessary.

All the other types in TypeScript belong to one of the following categories:

- **Primitive types**: This includes Number, String, Boolean, Void, Null, Undefined, and Enum types.

- **Union types**: Union types are out of the scope of this book. You can take a look at them in the specification of TypeScript.

- **Object types**: This includes Function types, classes and interface type references, array types, tuple types, function types, and constructor types.

- **Type parameters**: This includes Generics that are going to be described in the *Writing generic code by using type parameters* section.

Understanding the Primitive types

Most of the primitive types in TypeScript are the ones we are already familiar with in JavaScript: Number, String, Boolean, Null, and Undefined. So, we are going to skip their formal explanation here. Another set of types that is handy while developing Angular 2 applications is the Enum types defined by users.

The Enum types

The Enum types are primitive user-defined types that, according to the specification, are subclasses of Number. The concept of `enums` exists in the Java, C++, and C# languages, and it has the same semantics in TypeScript—user-defined types consisting of sets of named values called elements. In TypeScript, we can define `enum` using the following syntax:

```
enum STATES {
  CONNECTING,
  CONNECTED,
  DISCONNECTING,
  WAITING,
  DISCONNECTED
};
```

This is going to be translated to the following JavaScript:

```
var STATES;
(function (STATES) {
```

```
    STATES[STATES["CONNECTING"] = 0] = "CONNECTING";
    STATES[STATES["CONNECTED"] = 1] = "CONNECTED";
    STATES[STATES["DISCONNECTING"] = 2] = "DISCONNECTING";
    STATES[STATES["WAITING"] = 3] = "WAITING";
    STATES[STATES["DISCONNECTED"] = 4] = "DISCONNECTED";
})(STATES || (STATES = {}));
```

We can use the enum type as follows:

```
if (this.state === STATES.CONNECTING) {
  console.log('The system is connecting');
}
```

Understanding the Object types

In this section, we're going to take a look at the Array types and Function types, which belong to the more generic class of Object types. We will also explore how we can define classes and interfaces. Tuple types were introduced by TypeScript 1.3, and their main purpose is to allow the language to begin typing the new features introduced by ES2015, such as destructuring. We will not describe them in this book. For further reading you can take a look at the language's specification at http://www.typescriptlang.org.

The Array types

In TypeScript, arrays are JavaScript arrays with a common element type. This means that we cannot have elements from different types in a given array. We have different array types for all the built-in types in TypeScript, plus all the custom types that we define.

We can define an array of numbers as follows:

```
let primes: number[] = [];
primes.push(2);
primes.push(3);
```

If we want to have an array, which seems heterogeneous, similar to the arrays in JavaScript, we can use the type reference to any:

```
let randomItems: any[] = [];
randomItems.push(1);
randomItems.push("foo");
randomItems.push([]);
randomItems.push({});
```

This is possible, since the types of all the values we're pushing to the array are subtypes of the any type and the array we've declared contains values of the type any.

We can use the array methods we're familiar with in JavaScript with all the TypeScript Array types:

```
let randomItems: any[] = [];
randomItems.push("foo");
randomItems.push("bar");
randomItems.join(''); // foobar
randomItems.splice(1, 0, "baz");
randomItems.join(''); // foobazbar
```

We also have the square-brackets operator that gives us random access to the array's elements:

```
let randomItems: any[] = [];
randomItems.push("foo");
randomItems.push("bar");
randomItems[0] === "foo"
randomItems[1] === "bar"
```

The Function types

The function types are a set of all the functions with different signatures, including the different number of arguments, different arguments' types, or different types of the return result.

We're already familiar with how to create a new function in JavaScript. We can use function expression or function declaration:

```
// function expression
var isPrime = function (n) {
  // body
};
// function declaration
function isPrime(n) {
  // body
};
```

Or, we can use the new arrow function syntax:

```
var isPrime = n => {
  // body
};
```

The only thing TypeScript alters is the feature to define the types of the function's arguments and the type of its return result. After the compiler of the language performs its type checking and transpilation, all the type annotations will be removed. If we use function expression and we assign a function to a variable, we will be able to define the variable type in the following way:

```
let variable: (arg1: type1, arg2: type2, ..., argn: typen) => returnType
```

For example:

```
let isPrime: (n: number) => boolean = n => {
  // body
};
```

In case of `function declaration`, we'll have:

```
function isPrime(n: number): boolean {
  // body
}
```

If we want to define a method in a object literal, we can process it in the following way:

```
let math = {
  squareRoot(n: number): number {
    // ...
  },
};
```

In the preceding example, we defined an object literal using the ES2015 syntax that defines the method `squareRoot`.

In case we want to define a function that produces some side effects instead of returning a result, we can define it as a `void` function:

```
let person = {
  _name: null,
  setName(name: string): void {
    this._name = name;
  }
};
```

Defining classes

TypeScript classes are similar to what ES2015 offers. However, it alters the type declarations and creates more syntax sugar. For example, let's take the Human class we defined earlier and make it a valid TypeScript class:

```
class Human {
  static totalPeople = 0;
  _name: string;
  constructor(name) {
    this._name = name;
    Human.totalPeople += 1;
  }
  get name() {
    return this._name;
  }
  set name(val) {
    this._name = val;
  }
  talk() {
    return `Hi, I'm ${this.name}!`;
  }
}
```

There is no difference between the current TypeScript definition with the one we already introduced, however, in this case the declaration of the _name property is mandatory. Here is how we can use the class:

```
let human = new Human('foo');
console.log(human._name);
```

Using access modifiers

Similarly, for most conventional object-oriented languages that support classes, TypeScript allows definition of access modifiers. In order to deny direct access to the _name property outside the class it is defined in, we can declare it as private:

```
class Human {
  static totalPeople = 0;
  private _name: string;
  // ...
}
```

The supported access modifiers by TypeScript are:

- **Public**: All the properties and methods declared as public could be accessed anywhere.

- **Private**: All the properties and methods declared as private can be accessed only from inside the class' definition itself.

- **Protected**: All the properties and methods declared as protected can be accessed from inside the class' definition or the definition of any other class extending the one that owns the property or the method.

Access modifiers are a great way to implement Angular 2 services with good encapsulation and a well-defined interface. In order to understand it better, let's take a look at an example using the class' hierarchy defined earlier, which is ported to TypeScript:

```
class Human {
  static totalPeople = 0;
  constructor(protected name: string, private age: number) {
    Human.totalPeople += 1;
  }
  talk() {
    return `Hi, I'm ${this.name}!`;
  }
}

class Developer extends Human {
  constructor(name: string, private languages: string[], age: number)
{
    super(name, age);
  }
  talk() {
    return `${super.talk()} And I know ${this.languages.join(', ')}.`;
  }
}
```

Just like ES2015, TypeScript supports the `extends` keyword and desugars it to the prototypal JavaScript inheritance.

In the preceding example, we set the access modifiers of the `name` and `age` properties directly inside the constructor function. The semantics behind this syntax differs from the one used in the previous example. It has the following meaning: define a protected property called `name` of the type `string` and assign the first value passed to the constructor call to it. It is the same for the private `age` property. This saves us from explicitly setting the value in the constructor itself. If we take a look at the constructor of the `Developer` class, we can see that we can use the mixture between these syntaxes. We can explicitly define the property in the constructor's signature or we can only define that the constructor accepts the parameters of the given types.

Now, let's create a new instance of the `Developer` class:

```
let dev = new Developer("foo", ["JavaScript", "Go"], 42);
dev.languages = ["Java"];
```

During compilation, TypeScript will throw an error telling us that **Property languages is private and only accessible inside class "Developer"**. Now, let's see what's going to happen if we create a new `Human` class and try to access its properties from outside its definition:

```
let human = new Human("foo", 42);
human.age = 42;
human.name = "bar";
```

In this case, we'll get the following two errors:

Property age is private and is only accessible inside class "Human" and the **Property name is a protected and only accessible inside class "Human" and its subclasses**.

However, if we try to access the _name property from inside the definition of `Developer`, the compiler won't throw any errors.

In order to get a better sense of what the TypeScript compiler will produce out of a type annotated class, let's take a look at the JavaScript produced by the following definition:

```
class Human {
  constructor(private name: string) {}
}
```

The resulting ECMAScript 5 will be:

```
var Human = (function () {
    function Human(name) {
        this.name = name;
    }
    return Human;
})();
```

The defined property is added directly to the objects instantiated by calling the constructor function with the operator `new`. This means that once the code is compiled, we can directly access the private members of the created objects. In order to wrap this up, access modifiers are added in the language in order to help us enforce better encapsulation and get compile-time errors in case we violate it.

Defining interfaces

Subtyping in programming languages allows us to treat objects in the same way based on the observation that they are specialized versions of a generic object. This doesn't mean that they have to be instances of the same class of objects, or that they have complete intersection between their interfaces. The objects might have only a few common properties and still be treated the same way in a specific context. In JavaScript, we usually use duck typing. We may invoke specific methods for all the objects passed to a function based on the assumption that these methods exist. However, all of us have experienced the *undefined is not a function* error thrown by the JavaScript interpreter.

Object-oriented programming and TypeScript come with a solution. They allow us to make sure our objects have similar behavior if they implement interfaces that declare the subset of the properties they own.

For example, we can define our interface `Accountable`:

```
interface Accountable {
  getIncome(): number;
}
```

Now, we can make sure both `Individual` and `Firm` implement this interface by doing as follows:

```
class Firm implements Accountable {
  getIncome(): number {
    // ...
  }
}
class Individual implements Accountable {
  getIncome(): number {
    // ...
  }
}
```

In case we implement a given interface, we need to provide implementation for all the methods defined inside it, otherwise the TypeScript compiler will throw an error. The methods we implement must have the same signature as the ones declared in the interface definition.

TypeScript interfaces also support properties. In the `Accountable` interface, we can include a field called `accountNumber` with a type of string:

```
interface Accountable {
  accountNumber: string;
  getIncome(): number;
}
```

We can define it in our class as a field or a getter.

Interface inheritance

Interfaces may also extend each other. For example, we may turn our `Individual` class into an interface that has a social security number:

```
interface Accountable {
  accountNumber: string;
  getIncome(): number;
}
interface Individual extends Accountable {
  ssn: string;
}
```

Since interfaces support multiple inheritances, `Individual` may also extend the interface `Human` that has the `name` and `age` properties:

```
interface Accountable {
  accountNumber: string;
  getIncome(): number;
}
interface Human {
  age: number;
  name: number;
}
interface Individual extends Accountable, Human {
  ssn: string;
}
```

Implementing multiple interfaces

In case the class's behavior is a union of the properties defined in a couple of interfaces, it may implement all of them:

```
class Person implements Human, Accountable {
  age: number;
  name: string;
```

```
accountNumber: string;
getIncome(): number {
  // ...
}
}
```

In this case, we need to provide the implementation of all the methods declared inside the interfaces our class implements, otherwise the compiler will throw a compile-time error.

Further expressiveness with TypeScript decorators

In ES2015, we are able to decorate only classes, properties, methods, getters, and setters. TypeScript takes this further by allowing us to decorate functions or method parameters:

```
class Http {
  // ...
}
class GitHubApi {
  constructor(@Inject(Http) http) {
    // ...
  }
}
```

However, the parameter decorators should not alter any additional behavior. Instead, they are used to generate metadata. The most typical use case of these decorators is the dependency injection mechanism of Angular 2.

Writing generic code by using type parameters

In the beginning of the section on using static typing, we mentioned the type parameters. In order to get a better understanding of them, let's begin with an example. Let's suppose we want to implement the classical data-structure BinarySearchTree. Let's define its interface using a class without applying any method implementations:

```
class Node {
  value: any;
  left: Node;
```

```
      right: Node;
  }

  class BinarySearchTree {
    private root: Node;
    insert(any: value): void { /* … */ }
    remove(any: value): void { /* … */ }
    exists(any: value): boolean { /* … */ }
    inorder(callback: {(value: any): void}): void { /* … */ }
  }
```

In the preceding snippet, we defined a class called Node. The instances of this class represent the individual nodes in our tree. Each node has a left and a right child node and a value of the type any; we use any in order to be able to store data of any type inside our nodes and respectively inside BinarySearchTree.

Although the earlier implementation looks reasonable, we're giving up on using the most important feature that TypeScript provides—static typing. By using any as a type of the value field inside the Node class, we can't take complete advantage of the compile-time type checking. This also limits the features that IDEs and text editors provide when we access the value property of the instances of the Node class.

TypeScript comes with an elegant solution that is already widely popular in the world of static typing—type parameters. Using generics, we can parameterize the classes we create with the type parameters. For example, we can turn our Node class into the following:

```
  class Node<T> {
    value: T;
    left: Node<T>;
    right: Node<T>;
  }
```

Node<T> indicates that this class has a single type parameter called T that is used somewhere inside the class's definition. We can use Node by doing as follows:

```
  let numberNode = new Node<number>();
  let stringNode = new Node<string>();
  numberNode.right = new Node<number>();
  numberNode.value = 42;
  numberNode.value = "42"; // Type "string" is not assignable to type
  "number"
  numberNode.left = stringNode; // Type Node<string> is not assignable
  to type Node<number>
```

In the preceding snippet, we created three nodes: `numberNode`, `stringNode`, and another node of the type `Node<number>`, assigning its value to the right child of `numberNode`. Notice that since `numberNode` is of the type `Node<number>`, we can set its value to `42`, but we can't use the string `"42"`. The same is applicable to its left child. In the definition, we've explicitly declared that we want the left and right children to be of the type `Node<number>`. This means that we cannot assign values of the type `Node<string>` to them; that's why we get the second compile-time error.

Using generic functions

Another typical use of generics is for defining functions that operate over a set of types. For example, we may define an `identity` function that accepts an argument of type `T` and returns it:

```
function identity<T>(arg: T) {
  return arg;
}
```

However, in some cases, we may want to use only the instances of the types that have some specific properties. For achieving this, we can use an extended syntax that allows us to declare subtypes of the types that should be the type parameters:

```
interface Comparable {
  compare(a: Comparable): number;
}
function sort<T extends Comparable>(arr: Comparable[]): Comparable[] {
  // ...
}
```

For example, here, we defined an interface called `Comparable`. It has a single operation called `compare`. The classes that implement the interface `Comparable` need to implement the operation `compare`. When `compare` is called with a given argument, it returns `1` if the target object is bigger than the passed argument, `0` if they are equal, and `-1` if the target object is smaller than the passed argument.

Having multiple type parameters

TypeScript allows us to use multiple type parameters:

```
class Pair<K, V> {
  key: K;
  value: V;
}
```

In this case, we can create an instance of the class `Pair<K, V>` using the following syntax:

```
let pair = new Pair<string, number>();
pair.key = "foo";
pair.value = 42;
```

Writing less verbose code with TypeScript's type inference

Static typing has a number of benefits; however, it makes us write a more verbose code by adding all the required type annotations.

In some cases, the TypeScript's compiler is able to guess the types of expressions inside our code, for instance:

```
let answer = 42;
answer = "42"; // Type "string" is not assignable to type "number"
```

In the preceding example, we defined a variable `answer` and we assigned the value `42` to it. Since TypeScript is statically typed and the type of a variable cannot change once declared, the compiler is smart enough to guess that the type of `answer` is `number`.

If we don't assign a value to a variable within its definition, the compiler will set its type to `any`:

```
let answer;
answer = 42;
answer = "42";
```

The preceding snippet will compile without any compile-time errors.

Best common type

Sometimes, the type inference could be a result of several expressions. Such is the case when we assign a heterogeneous array to a variable:

```
let x = ["42", 42];
```

In this case, the type of x will be `any[]`. However, suppose we have the following:

```
let x = [42, null, 32];
```

The type of x will then be `number[]`, since the type `Number` is a subtype of `Null`.

Contextual type inference

Contextual typing occurs when the type of an expression is implied from its location, for example:

```
document.body.addEventListener("mousedown", e => {
  e.foo(); // Property "foo" does not exists on a type "MouseEvent"
}, false);
```

In this case, the type of the argument of the callback e is *guessed* by the compiler based on the context in which it is used. The compiler understands what the type of e is based on the call of addEventListener and the arguments passed to the method. In case we were using a keyboard event (keydown, for example), TypeScript would have been aware that e is of the type KeyboardEvent.

Type inference is a mechanism that allows us to write less verbose code by taking advantage of the static analysis performed by TypeScript. Based on the context, TypeScript's compiler is able to guess the type of a given expression without explicit definition.

Using ambient type definitions

Although static typing is amazing, most of the frontend libraries we use are built with JavaScript, which is dynamically typed. Since we'd want to use TypeScript in Angular 2, not having type definitions in the code that uses external JavaScript libraries is a big issue; it prevents us from taking advantage of the compile-time type-checking.

TypeScript was built keeping these points in mind. In order to allow the TypeScript compiler to take care of what it does best, we can use the so-called ambient type definitions. They allow us to provide external type definitions of the existing JavaScript libraries. This way, they provide hints to the compiler.

Using predefined ambient type definitions

Fortunately, we don't have to create ambient type definitions for all JavaScript libraries and frameworks we use. The community and/or the authors of these libraries have already published such definitions online; the biggest repository resides at: https://github.com/DefinitelyTyped/DefinitelyTyped. There's also a tool for managing them called **typings**. We can install it using npm by the following command:

```
npm install -g typings
```

Make sure that you have the proper version of typings install by running:

```
typings -v
1.0.4
```

The configuration of typings is defined in a file called typings.json and all installed ambient typings, by default, will be in the directory ./typings.

In order to create typings.json file with basic configuration use:

```
typings init
```

We can install new type definition using:

```
typings install dt~angularjs --global
```

The preceding command will download the type definitions for AngularJS 1.x and save them in globals/angular/angular.d.ts under the typings directory.

In order to download a type definition and add entry for it inside typings.json you can use:

```
typings install dt~angular --global --save
```

After running the preceding command your typings.json file should look similar to:

```
{
  "dependencies": {},
  "devDependencies": {},
  "globalDependencies": {
    "angular": "github:DefinitelyTyped/DefinitelyTyped/angularjs/angul
ar.d.ts#1c4a34873c9e70cce86edd0e61c559e43dfa5f75"
  }
}
```

Now in order to use AngularJS 1.x with TypeScript create app.ts and enter the following content:

```
/// <reference path="./typings/index.d.ts"/>

var module = angular.module("module", []);
module.controller("MainCtrl",
  function MainCtrl($scope: angular.IScope) {

  });
```

To compile `app.ts` use:

```
tsc app.ts
```

The TypeScript compile will output the compiled content into `app.js`. In order to add extra automation and invoke the TypeScript compiler each time you change any of the files in your project, you can use a task runner like gulp or grunt, or pass the `-w` option to `tsc`.

 At the moment of writing, Microsoft is working on a standard way of managing type definitions. For further information, you can take a look at the following link `https://blogs.msdn.microsoft.com/typescript/2016/06/15/the-future-of-declaration-files/`.

 Since using the reference element for including type definitions is considered bad practice we can use a `tsconfig.json` file instead. There we can configure which directories need to be included in the compilation process by `tsc`. For more information visit `https://github.com/Microsoft/TypeScript/wiki/tsconfig.json`.

Custom ambient type definitions

To understand how everything works together, let's take a look at an example. Suppose we have the following interface of a JavaScript library:

```
var DOM = {
  // Returns a set of elements which match the passed selector
  selectElements: function (selector) {
    // …
  },
  hide: function (element) {
    // …
  },
  show: function (element) {
    // …
  }
};
```

We have an object literal assigned to a variable called DOM. The object has the following methods:

- selectElements: Accepts a single argument with type string and returns a set of DOM elements.

- hide: Accepts a DOM node as an argument and returns nothing.

- show: Accepts a DOM node as an argument and returns nothing.

In TypeScript, the preceding definition would look as follows:

```
var DOM = {
  // Returns a set of elements which match the passed selector
  selectElements: function (selector: string): HTMLElement[] {
    return [];
  },
  hide: function (element: HTMLElement): void {
    element.hidden = true;
  },
  show: function (element: HTMLElement): void {
    element.hidden = false;
  }
};
```

This means that we can define our library's interface as follows:

```
interface LibraryInterface {
  selectElements(selector: string): HTMLElement[]
  hide(element: HTMLElement): void
  show(element: HTMLElement): void
}
```

Defining d.ts files

After we have the interface of our library, it will be easy to create the ambient type definition; we just have to create a file with an extension d.ts called dom and enter the following content:

```
// inside "dom.d.ts"

interface DOMLibraryInterface {
  selectElements(selector: string): HTMLElement[]
  hide(element: HTMLElement): void
  show(element: HTMLElement): void
}

declare var DOM: DOMLibraryInterface;
```

In the preceding snippet, we defined the interface called `DOMLibraryInterface` and declared the variable `DOM` of the type `DOMLibraryInterface`.

The only thing left before being able to exploit static typing with our JavaScript library is including the external type definition in the script files we want to use our library in. We can do it as follows:

```
/// <reference path="dom.d.ts"/>
```

The preceding snippet hints the compiler on where to find the ambient type definitions.

Summary

In this chapter, we peeked at the TypeScript language that is used for the implementation of Angular 2. Although we can develop our Angular 2 applications using ECMAScript 5, Google's recommendation is to use TypeScript in order to take advantage of the static typing it provides.

While exploring the language, we looked at some of the core features of ES2015 and ES2016. We explained the ES2015 and ES2016 classes, arrow functions, block scope variable definitions, destructuring, and modules. Since Angular 2 takes advantage of the ES2016 decorators and more accurately their extension in TypeScript, a section was dedicated to them.

After this, we took a look at how we can take advantage of static typing by using explicit type definitions. We described some of the built-in types in TypeScript and how we can define classes in the language by specifying access modifiers for their members. Our next stop was the interfaces. We ended our adventures in TypeScript by explaining the type parameters and the ambient type definitions.

In the next chapter, we are going to start exploring Angular 2 in depth by using the framework's components and directives.

4
Getting Started with Angular 2 Components and Directives

By this point, you're already familiar with the core building blocks that Angular 2 provides for the development of single-page applications and the relations between them. However, we've touched only the surface by introducing the general idea behind Angular's concepts and the basic syntax used for their definition. In this chapter, we'll take a deep dive into Angular 2's components and directives.

In the following sections, we will cover these topics:

- Enforced separation of concerns of the building blocks that Angular 2 provides for developing applications.
- The appropriate use of directives or components when interacting with the DOM.
- Built-in directives and developing custom ones.
- An in-depth look at components and their templates.
- Content projection.
- View children versus content children.
- The component's life cycle.
- Using template references.
- Configuring Angular's change detection.

The Hello world! application in Angular 2

Now, let's build our first "Hello world!" app in Angular 2! In order to get everything up and running as easy and quickly as possible, for our first application, we will use the ECMAScript 5 syntax with the transpiled bundle of Angular 2. First, create the index.html file with the following content:

```html
<!-- ch4/es5/hello-world/index.html -->

<!DOCTYPE html>
<html lang="en">
<head>
  <meta charset="UTF-8">
  <title></title>
</head>
<body>
  <script src="https://npmcdn.com/zone.js@0.6.12/dist/zone.js"></script>
  <script src="https://npmcdn.com/reflect-metadata@0.1.3/Reflect.js"></script>
  <script src="https://npmcdn.com/rxjs/bundles/Rx.umd.js"></script>
  <script src="https://npmcdn.com/@angular/core/bundles/core.umd.js"></script>
  <script src="https://npmcdn.com/@angular/common/bundles/common.umd.js"></script>
  <script src="https://npmcdn.com/@angular/compiler/bundles/compiler.umd.js"></script>
  <script src="https://npmcdn.com/@angular/platform-browser/bundles/platform-browser.umd.js"></script>
  <script src="https://npmcdn.com/@angular/platform-browser-dynamic/bundles/platform-browser-dynamic.umd.js"></script>
  <script src="./app.js"></script>
</body>
</html>
```

The preceding HTML file defines the basic structure of our page. Just before closing the body tag, we have references to four script files: the polyfills required by the framework (including zone.js and others), RxJS, the ES5 bundle of Angular 2, and the file that contains the application we're going to build.

 RxJS is used by Angular's core in order to allow us to empower the reactive programming paradigm in our applications. In the following content, we will take only a shallow look at how we can take advantage of observables. For further information, you can visit the RxJS GitHub repository at https://github.com/ReactiveX/rxjs.

In the same directory where your `index.html` resides, create a file called `app.js` and enter the following content inside it:

```
// ch4/es5/hello-world/app.js

var App = ng.core.Component({
  selector: 'app',
  template: '<h1>Hello {{target}}!</h1>'
})
.Class({
  constructor: function () {
    this.target = 'world';
  }
});

ng.platformBrowserDynamic.bootstrap(App);
```

In the preceding snippet, we define a component called `App` with an `app` selector. This selector will match all the app elements inside our templates that are in the scope of the application. The component has the following template:

```
'<h1>Hello {{target}}!</h1>'
```

This syntax should already be familiar to you from AngularJS 1.x. When compiled in the context of the given component, the preceding snippet will interpolate the template with the result of the expression inside the curly brackets. In our case, the expression is simply the `target` variable.

To `Class`, we pass an object literal, which has a single method called `constructor`. This DSL provides an alternative way to define classes in ECMAScript 5. In the body of the `constructor` function, we add a property called `target` with a value of the `"world"` string. In the last line of the snippet, we invoke the `bootstrap` method in order to initialize our application with `App` as a root component.

Note that `bootstrap` is located under `ng.platformBrowserDynamic`. This is due to the fact that the framework is built for different platforms in mind, such as a browser, NativeScript, and so on. By placing the `bootstrap` methods used by the different platforms under a separate namespace, Angular 2 can implement different logic to initialize the application and also include different sets of providers and directives that are platform specific.

Now, if you open `index.html` with your browser, you should see some errors, as shown in the following screenshot:

This happened because we missed something quite important. We didn't use the root component anywhere inside `index.html`. In order to finish the application, add the following HTML element after the open tag of the body element:

```
<app></app>
```

Now, you can refresh your browser to see the following result:

Using TypeScript

Although we already have an Angular 2 application running, we can do much better! We didn't use any package manager or module loader. We spent all of *Chapter 3, TypeScript Crash Course*, talking about TypeScript; however, we didn't write a single line of it in the preceding application. Although it is not required that you use TypeScript with Angular 2, it's much convenient to take advantage of all the bonuses that static typing provides.

Setting up our environment

The core team of Angular developed a brand new CLI tool for Angular 2, which allows us to bootstrap our applications with a few commands. Although we are going to introduce it in the last chapter, by then, in order to boost our learning experience, we are going to use the code located at https://github.com/mgechev/switching-to-angular2. It includes all the examples in this book and allows us to quickly bootstrap our Angular 2 application (you can know more on how to quickly start developing web applications with Angular 2 in *Chapter 5, Dependency Injection in Angular 2.*). It has all the required dependencies declared in package.json, the definition of basic gulp tasks, such as the development server, the transpilation of your TypeScript code to ECMAScript 5, live-reload, and so on. Our upcoming examples are going to be based on it.

In order to set up the switching-to-angular2 project, you'll need Git, Node.js v5.x.x, and npm up and running on your computer. If you have a different version of the Node.js installed, I recommend that you take a look at nvm (the Node.js version manager, which is available at https://www.npmjs.com/package/nvm) or n (https://www.npmjs.com/package/n). Using these tools, you'll be able to have multiple versions of Node.js on your machine and switch between them with a single command via the command line.

Installing our project repository

Let's start by setting up the switching-to-angular2 project. Open your terminal and enter the following commands:

```
# Will clone the repository and save it to directory called
# switching-to-angular2
git clone https://github.com/mgechev/switching-to-angular2.git
cd switching-to-angular2
npm install
```

The first line will clone the switching-to-angular2 project into a directory called switching-to-angular2.

The last step before being able to run the seed project is to install all the required dependencies using npm. This step may take a while depending on your Internet connection, so be patient and do not interrupt it. If you encounter any problems, do not hesitate to raise the issues at https://github.com/mgechev/switching-to-angular2/issues.

The last step left is to start the development server:

```
npm start
```

When the process of the transpilation is completed, your browser will automatically open with this URL: `http://localhost:5555/dist/dev`. You should now see a view similar to what is shown in the following screenshot:

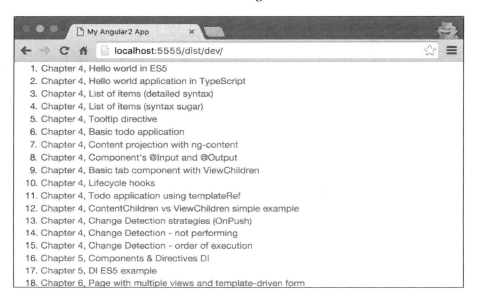

Playing with Angular 2 and TypeScript

Now, let's play around with the files we already have! Navigate to the `app/ch4/ts/hello-world` directory inside `switching-to-angular2`. Then, open `app.ts` and replace its content with the following snippet:

```
// ch4/ts/hello-world/app.ts

import {Component} from '@angular/core';
import {bootstrap} from '@angular/platform-browser-dynamic';

@Component({
  selector: 'app',
  templateUrl: './app.html'
})
class App {
```

```
    target: string;
    constructor() {
      this.target = 'world';
    }
}

bootstrap(App);
```

Let's take a look at the code line by line:

```
import {Component} from '@angular/core';
import {bootstrap} from '@angular/platform-browser-dynamic';
```

Initially, we import the @Component decorator from the @angular/core module and the bootstrap function from @angular/platform-browser-dynamic. Later, we use @Component to decorate the App class. To the @Component decorator, we pass almost the same object literal that we used in the ECMAScript 5 version of the application, and this way, we define the CSS selector for the component.

As a next step, we define the view of the component. However, note that in this case, we use templateUrl instead of simply inlining the component's template.

Open app.html and replace the file's content with <h1>Hello {{target}}!</h1>. The content of app.html should be the same as the inlined template we used previously. Since we can use a template by both inlining it (with template) and setting its URL (templateUrl), the component's API is quite similar to the AngularJS 1.x directives API.

In the last line of the snippet, we bootstrap the application by providing the root component.

Digging into the index

Now, let's take a look at index.html in order to get a sense of what goes on when we start the application:

```html
<!-- ch4/ts/hello-world/index.html -->
<!DOCTYPE html>
<html lang="en">
<head>
  <meta charset="utf-8">
  <meta http-equiv="X-UA-Compatible" content="IE=edge">
  <title><%= TITLE %></title>
  <meta name="description" content="">
  <meta name="viewport" content="width=device-width, initial-scale=1">
```

```
  <!-- inject:css -->
  <!-- endinject -->
</head>
<body>
  <app>Loading...</app>
  <!-- inject:js -->
  <!-- endinject -->
  <%= INIT %>
</body>
</html>
```

Note that inside the body of the page, we use the app element with the content of the text node, "Loading...", inside. The "Loading..." label will be visible until the application gets bootstrapped and the main component gets rendered.

 There are template placeholders <%= INIT %> and <-- inject:js... that inject content that is specific to individual demos. They are not Angular specific but instead aim to prevent code duplications in the code samples attached to the book because of the shared structure between them. In order to see how this specific HTML file has been transformed, open /dist/dev/ch4/ts/hello-world/index.html.

Using Angular 2 directives

We already built our simple "Hello world!" app. Now, let's start building something that is closer to a real-life application. By the end of this section, we'll have a simple application that lists a number of items we need to do and greets us at the header of the page.

Let's start by developing our app component. The two modifications from the previous example that we need to make are to rename the target property to name and add a list of todos to the component's controller definition:

```
// ch4/ts/ng-for/detailed-syntax/app.ts

import {Component} from '@angular/core';
import {bootstrap} from '@angular/platform-browser-dynamic';

@Component({
  selector: 'app',
  templateUrl: './app.html',
})
```

```
class App {
  todos: string[];
  name: string;
  constructor() {
    this.name = 'John';
    this.todos = ['Buy milk', 'Save the world'];
  }
}
bootstrap(App);
```

The only thing left is to change the template in order to consume the provided data. We're already familiar with the `ng-repeat` directive from AngularJS 1.x. It allows us to loop a list of items using a microsyntax, which is later interpreted by AngularJS 1.x. However, the directive doesn't carry enough semantics, so it is hard to build tools that perform static code analysis and help us improve our development experience. Since the `ng-repeat` directive is quite useful, Angular 2 took the idea and improved it further in order to allow more sophisticated tooling by introducing further semantics on top of it. It allows better static code analysis to be performed by IDEs and text editors. Such support will prevent us from making typos in the code we write and allow us to have smoother development experience.

In `app.html`, add the following content:

```
<!-- ch4/ts/ng-for/detailed-syntax/app.html -->

<h1>Hello {{name}}!</h1>
<p>

  Here's a list of the things you need to do:
</p>
<ul>
  <template ngFor let-todo [ngForOf]="todos">
    <li>{{todo}}</li>
  </template>
</ul>
```

 The `template` element is a place where we can hold markup and make sure that it won't be rendered by the browser. This is quite useful if we need to embed the templates of our application directly into the markup of the page and let the template engine we're using to process them later. In the current example, this means that if the Angular 2 DOM compiler doesn't process the DOM tree, all we're going to see on the screen are the h1, p elements and the ul element without any list items.

Now, after you refresh your browser, you should see the following result:

So far, so good! The only new things left in the preceding snippets are the attributes of the `template` element that we're not familiar with, such as `ngFor`, `let-todo`, and `[ngForOf]`. Let's take a look at them.

The ngFor directive

The `ngFor` directive is a directive that allows us to loop over a collection of items and does exactly what `ng-repeat` does in AngularJS 1.x, but it brings some extra semantics. Note that the `ngForOf` attribute is surrounded by brackets. At first, these brackets might seem like invalid HTML. However, according to the HTML specification, their use is permitted in attribute names. The only thing the W3C validator is going to complain about is the fact that the `template` element doesn't own such attributes; however, browsers won't have problems processing the markup.

The semantics behind these brackets is that the value of the attribute surrounded by them is an expression, which needs to be evaluated.

Improved semantics of the directives syntax

In *Chapter 1, Getting Started with Angular 2*, we mentioned the opportunity for improved tooling in Angular 2. A big issue in AngularJS 1.x is the different ways in which we can use directives. This requires an understanding of the attribute values, which can be literals, expressions, callbacks, or a microsyntax. Angular 2 eliminates this problem by introducing a few simple conventions that are built into the framework:

- `propertyName="value"`

- `[propertyName]="expression"`
- `(eventName)="handler()"`

In the first line, the `propertyName` attribute accepts a string literal as a value. Angular will not process the attribute's value any further; it will use it the way it is set in the template.

The second syntax, `[propertyName]="expression"`, gives a hint to Angular 2 that the value of the attributes should be handled as an expression. When Angular 2 finds an attribute surrounded by brackets, it will interpret the expression in the context of the component associated to the template. In short, if we want to set a non-string value or result of an expression as value of given property we need to use this syntax.

The last example shows how we can bind to events. The semantics behind `(eventName)="handler()"` is that we want to handle all events called `eventName` that are triggered by the given component with the `handler()` expression.

We're going to discuss more examples later in this chapter.

Angular provides alternative canonical syntax, which allows us to define the bindings of the elements without using brackets. For instance, the property binding can be expressed using the following code:

```
<input [value]="foo">
```

It can also be expressed using this:

```
<input bind-value="foo">
```

Similarly, we can express the event bindings with the following code:

```
<button (click)="handle()">Click me</button>
```

They can also be expressed using this:

```
<button on-click="handle()">Click me</button>
```

Declaring variables inside a template

The last thing left from the preceding template is the `let-todo` attribute. What we are telling Angular using this syntax is that we want to declare a new variable called `todo` and bind it to the individual items from the collection we get from the evaluation of the expression set as a value of `[ngForOf]`.

Using syntax sugar in templates

Although the template syntax is awesome and provides much more meaning of the code to the IDEs or text editors we use, it is quite verbose. Angular 2 provides an alternative syntax, which will be desugared to the one shown in the preceding.

There are a few Angular 2 directives that require the usage of a template element, for example, `ngForOf`, `ngIf`, and `ngSwitch`. Since such directives are used often, there's an alternative syntax for them. Instead of typing down the entire template element explicitly, we can simply prefix the directive with `*`. This will allow us to turn our `ngForOf` directive syntax usage into the following:

```html
<!-- ch4/ts/ng-for/syntax-sugar/app.html -->

<ul>
  <li *ngFor="let todo of todos">{{todo}}</li>
</ul>
```

Later, this template will be desugared by Angular 2 to the more verbose syntax described earlier. Since the less verbose syntax is easier to read and write, its use is considered as best practice.

> The `*` character allows you to remove the `template` element and put the directive directly on the root of the `template` element (in the preceding example, the list item, `li`).

Defining Angular 2 directives

Now that we've built a simple Angular 2 component, let's continue our journey by understanding the Angular 2 directives.

Using Angular 2 directives, we can apply different behavioral or structural changes over the DOM. In this example, we're going to build a simple tooltip directive.

In contrast to components, directives do not have views and templates, respectively. Another core difference between these two concepts is that the given HTML element may have only a single component but multiple directives on it. In other words, directives augment the elements compared to components that are the actual elements in our views.

Angular's core team's recommendation is to use directives as attributes, prefixed with a namespace. Keeping this in mind, we will use the tooltip directive in the following way:

```
<div saTooltip="Hello world!"></div>
```

In the preceding snippet, we use the tooltip directive over the div element. As a namespace, its selector uses the sa string.

> For simplicity, in the rest of the book we may not prefix all the selectors of our components and directives. However, for production applications following best practices is essential. You can find an Angular 2 style guide which points out such practices at https://angular.io/styleguide.

Before implementing our tooltip, we need to import a couple of things from @angular/core. Open a new TypeScript file called app.ts and enter the following content; we'll fill the placeholders later:

```
import {Directive, ElementRef, HostListener...} from '@angular/core';
```

In the preceding line, we import the following definitions:

- ElementRef: This allows us to inject the element reference (we're not limited to the DOM only) to the host element. In the sample usage of the preceding tooltip, we get an Angular wrapper of the div element, which holds the tooltip attribute.

- Directive: This decorator allows us to add the metadata required for the new directives we define.

- HostListener(eventname): This is a method decorator that accepts an event name as an argument. During initialization of the directive, Angular 2 will add the decorated method as an event handler for the eventname event of the host element.

Let's look at our implementation; this is what the directive's definition looks like:

```
// ch4/ts/tooltip/app.ts

@Directive({
  selector: '[saTooltip]'
})
export class Tooltip {
  @Input() saTooltip: string;

  constructor(private el: ElementRef, private overlay: Overlay) {
    this.overlay.attach(el.nativeElement);
  }
```

```
@HostListener('mouseenter')
onMouseEnter() {
  this.overlay.open(this.el, this.saTooltip);
}
@HostListener('mouseleave')
onMouseLeave() {
  this.overlay.close();
}
}
```

Setting the directive's inputs

In the preceding example, we declare a directive with the `saTooltip` selector. Note that Angular's HTML compiler is case sensitive, which means that it will distinguish the `[satooltip]` and `[saTooltip]` selectors. Later, we will declare the input of the directive using the `@Input` decorator over the `saTooltip` property. The semantics behind this code is: declare a property called `saTooltip` and bind it to the value of the result that we got from the evaluation of the expression passed to the `saTooltip` attribute.

The `@Input` decorator accepts a single argument—the name of the attribute we want to bind to. In case we don't pass an argument, Angular will create a binding between the attribute with the same name as the property itself. We will explain the concept of input and output in detail later in this chapter.

Understanding the directive's constructor

The constructor declares two private properties: `el` of the `ElementRef` type and `overlay` of the `Overlay` type. The `Overlay` class implements logic to manage the tooltips' overlays and is going to be injected using the DI mechanism of Angular. In order to declare it as available for injection, we need to declare the top-level component in the following way:

```
@Component({
  selector: 'app',
  templateUrl: './app.html',
  providers: [Overlay],
  // ...
})
class App {}
```

We're going to take a look at the dependency injection mechanism of Angular 2 in the next chapter, where we will explain the way in which we can declare the dependencies of our services, directives, and components.

The implementation of the Overlay class is not important for the purpose of this chapter. However, if you're interested in it, you can find the implementation in: ch4/ts/tooltip/app.ts.

Better encapsulation of directives

In order to make the tooltip directive available to the Angular's compiler, we need to explicitly declare where we intend to use it. For instance, take a look at the App class at ch4/ts/tooltip/app.ts; there, you can notice the following:

```
@Component({
  selector: 'app',
  templateUrl: './app.html',
  providers: [Overlay],
  directives: [Tooltip]
})
class App {}
```

To the @Component decorator, we pass an object literal that has the directives property. This property contains a list of all the directives that should be available in the entire component subtree with the root of the given component.

At first, it might seem annoying that you should explicitly declare all the directives that your component uses; however, this enforces better encapsulation. In AngularJS 1.x, all directives are in a global namespace. This means that all the directives defined in the application are accessible in all the templates. This brings in some problems, for example, name collision. In order to deal with this issue, we've introduced naming conventions, for instance, the "ng-" prefix of all the directives defined by AngularJS 1.x and "ui-" for all directives coming with the Angular UI.

This way, by explicitly declaring all the directives, the given component uses in Angular 2, we create a namespace specific to the individual components' subtrees (that is, the directives will be visible to the given root component and all of its successor components). Preventing name collisions is not the only benefit we get; it also helps us with better semantics of the code that we produce, since we're always aware of the directives accessible by the given component. We can find all the accessible directives of the given component by following the path from the component to the top of the component tree and taking the union of all the values of directives arrays set in the @ Component decorators. Given that components are extended from directives, we need to explicitly declare all the used components as well.

Since Angular 2 defines a set of built-in directives, the bootstrap method passes them in a similar way in order to make them available in the entire application in order to prevent us from code duplications. This list of predefined directives includes NgClass, NgFor, NgIf, NgStyle, NgSwitch, NgSwitchCase, and NgSwitchDefault. Their names are quite self-explanatory; we'll take a look at how we can use some of them later in this chapter.

Using Angular 2's built-in directives

Now, let's build a simple to-do application in order to demonstrate the syntax to define components further!

Our to-do items will have the following format:

```
interface Todo {
  completed: boolean;
  label: string;
}
```

Let's start by importing everything we are going to need:

```
import {Component, ViewEncapsulation} from '@angular/core';
import {bootstrap} from '@angular/platform-browser-dynamic';
```

Now, let's declare the component and the metadata associated with it:

```
@Component({
  selector: 'todo-app',
  templateUrl: './app.html',
  styles: [
    `ul li {
      list-style: none;
    }
```

```
    .completed {
      text-decoration: line-through;
    }`
  ],
  encapsulation: ViewEncapsulation.Emulated
})
```

Here, we specify that the selector of the `Todo` component will be the `todo-app` element. Later, we add the template URL, which points to the `app.html` file. After that, we use the `styles` property; this is the first time we encounter it. As we can guess from its name, it is used to set the styles of the component.

Introducing the component's view encapsulation

As we know, Angular 2 is inspired from Web Components, whose core feature is the shadow DOM. The shadow DOM allows us to encapsulate the styles of our Web Components without allowing them to leak outside the component's scope. Angular 2 provides this feature. If we want Angular's renderer to use the shadow DOM, we can use `ViewEncapsulation.Native`. However, the shadow DOM is not supported by all browsers; if we want to have the same level of encapsulation without using the shadow DOM, we can use `ViewEncapsulation.Emulated`. If we don't want to have any encapsulation at all, we can use `ViewEncapsulation.None`. By default, the renderer uses encapsulation of the type `Emulated`.

Implementing the component's controllers

Now, let's continue with the implementation of the application:

```
// ch4/ts/todo-app/app.ts
class TodoCtrl {
  todos: Todo[] = [{
    label: 'Buy milk',
    completed: false
  }, {
    label: 'Save the world',
    completed: false
  }];
  name: string = 'John';
  addTodo(label) { ... }
```

```
    removeTodo(idx) { … }
    toggleCompletion(idx) { … }
}
```

Here is part of the implementation of the controller associated with the template of the Todo application.

Inside the class declaration, we initialized the todos property to an array with two todo items:

```
{
  label: 'Buy milk',
  completed: false
}, {
  label: 'Save the world',
  completed: false
}
```

Now, let's update the template and render these items! Here's how this is done:

```
<ul>
  <li *ngFor="let todo of todos; let index = index" [class.
completed]="todo.completed">
    <input type="checkbox" [checked]="todo.completed"
      (change)="toggleCompletion(index)">
    {{todo.label}}
  </li>
</ul>
```

In the preceding template, we looped all the todo items inside the todos property of the controller. For each todo item, we created a checkbox that can toggle the item's completion status; we also rendered the todo item's label with the interpolation directive. Here, we can notice the syntax that was explained earlier:

- We bind to the change event of the checkbox using (change)="statement".
- We bind to the property of the todo item using [checked]="expr".

In order to have a line across the completed todo items, we bind to the class. completed property of the element. Since we want to apply the completed class to all the completed to-do items, we use [class.completed]="todo.completed". This way, we declare that we want to apply the completed class depending on the value of the todo.completed expression. Here is how our application looks now:

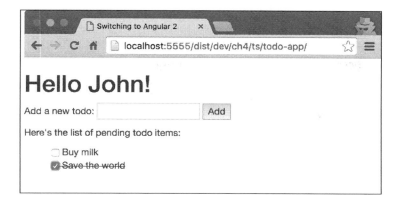

Similar to the class binding syntax, Angular allows us to bind to the element's styles and attributes. For instance, we can bind to the `td` element's `colspan` attribute using the following line of code:

```
<td [attr.colspan]="colspanCount"></td>
```

In the same way, we can bind to any `style` property using this line of code:

```
<div [style.backgroundImage]="expression"></td>
```

Handling user actions

So far, so good! Now, let's implement the `toggleCompletion` method. This method accepts the index of the to-do item as a single argument:

```
toggleCompletion(idx) {
  let todo = this.todos[idx];
  todo.completed = !todo.completed;
}
```

In `toggleCompletion`, we simply toggle the `completed` Boolean value associated with the current to-do item, which is specified by the index passed as an argument to the method.

Now, let's add a text input to add the new to-do items:

```
<p>
  Add a new todo:
  <input #newtodo type="text">
  <button (click)="addTodo(newtodo.value); newtodo.value = ''">
    Add
  </button>
</p>
```

The input here defines a new identifier called `newtodo`. We can reference the input using the `newtodo` identifier inside the template. Once the user clicks on the button, the `addTodo` method defined in the controller will be invoked with the value of the `newtodo` input as an argument. Inside the statement that is passed to the `(click)` attribute, we also reset the value of the `newtodo` input by setting it to the empty string.

 Note that directly manipulating DOM elements is not considered as best practice since it will prevent our component from running properly outside the browser environment. We will explain how we can migrate this application to Web Workers in *Chapter 8, Development Experience and Server-Side Rendering.*

Now, let's define the `addTodo` method:

```
addTodo(label) {
  this.todos.push({
    label,
    completed: false
  });
}
```

Inside it, we create a new to-do item using the object literal syntax.

The only thing left out of our application is to implement removal of existing to-do items. Since it is quite similar to the functionality used to toggle the completion of the to-do items, I'll leave its implementation as a simple exercise for the reader.

Using a directives' inputs and outputs

By refactoring our `todo` application, we are going to demonstrate how we can take advantage of the directives' inputs and outputs:

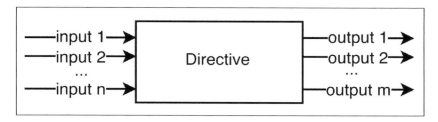

We can think of the inputs as properties (or even arguments) that the given directive accepts. The outputs could be considered as events that it triggers. When we use a directive provided by a third-party library, mostly we care about is its inputs and outputs because they define its API.

Inputs refers to values that parameterize the directive's behavior and/or view. On the other hand, outputs refers to events that the directive fires when something special happens.

Finding out directives' inputs and outputs

Now, let's divide our monolithic to-do application into separate components that communicate with each other. In the following screenshot, you can see the individual components that when composed together implement the functionality of the application:

The outer rectangle represents the entire Todo application. The first nested rectangle contains the component that is responsible for entering labels of the new to-do items, and the one below it lists the individual items that are stored in the root component.

Having said this, we can define these three components as follows:

- TodoApp: Responsible for maintaining the list of to-do items (adding new items and toggling the completion status).

- InputBox: Responsible for entering the label of the new to-do item. It has the following inputs and outputs:

  - Input: A placeholder for the textbox and a label for the submit button.

        °   `Output`: It should emit the content of the input once the submit button is clicked.

- `TodoList`: This is responsible for rendering the individual to-do items. It has the following inputs and outputs:

        °   `Input`: The list of to-do items.

        °   `Output`: Once the completion status of any of the to-do items changes, the component should emit the change.

Now, let's begin with the implementation!

Defining the component's inputs and outputs

Let's use a bottom-up approach and start with the `InputBox` component. Before that, we need a couple of imports from Angular's `@angular/core` package:

```
import {
  Component,
  Input,
  Output,
  EventEmitter
} from '@angular/core';
```

In the preceding code, we imported the `@Component`, `@Input`, and `@Output` decorators and the `EventEmitter` class. As their names state, `@Input` and `@Output` are used for declaring the directive's inputs and outputs. `EventEmitter` is a generic class (that is, accepting type parameter) which combined with the `@Output` decorator helps us emit outputs.

As the next step, let's take a look at the `InputBox` component's declaration:

```
// ch4/ts/inputs-outputs/app.ts

@Component({
  selector: 'text-input',
  template: `
    <input #todoInput [placeholder]="inputPlaceholder">
    <button (click)="emitText(todoInput.value);
                     todoInput.value = '';">
      {{buttonLabel}}
    </button>
  `
})
class InputBox {...}
```

Note that in the template, we declare a text input called `todoInput` and set its placeholder property to the value that we got from the evaluation of the `inputPlaceholder` expression. The value of the expression is the value of the `inputPlaceholder` property defined in the component's controller. This is the first input that we need to define:

```
class InputBox {
  @Input() inputPlaceholder: string;
  ...
}
```

Similarly, we declare the other input of the `buttonLabel` component, which we use as a value of the label of the button:

```
class InputBox {
  @Input() inputPlaceholder: string;
  @Input() buttonLabel: string;
  ...
}
```

In the preceding template, we bind the click event of the button to this expression: `emitText(todoInput.value); todoInput.value = '';`. The `emitText` method is supposed to be defined in the component's controller; once it is invoked, it should emit the value of the text input. Here is how we can implement this behavior:

```
class InputBox {
  ...
  @Output() inputText = new EventEmitter<string>();
  emitText(text: string) {
    this.inputText.emit(text);
  }
}
```

Initially, we declare an output called `inputText`. As its value, we set a new instance of the type `EventEmitter<string>` that we create.

 Note that all the outputs of all the components need to be instances of `EventEmitter`.

Inside the `emitText` method, we invoke the emit method of the `inputText` instance with the argument of the value of the text input.

Now, let's define the `TodoList` component in the same fashion:

```
@Component(...)
class TodoList {
  @Input() todos: Todo[];
  @Output() toggle = new EventEmitter<Todo>();
  toggleCompletion(index: number) {
    let todo = this.todos[index];
    this.toggle.emit(todo);
  }
}
```

Since the value of the object literal passed to the `@Component` decorator is not essential for the purpose of this section, we've omitted it. The complete implementation of this example could be found at `ch4/ts/inputs-outputs/app.ts`. Let's take a look at the body of the `TodoList` class. Similarly, for the `InputBox` component, we define the `todos` input. We also define the `toggle` output by declaring the `toggle` property, setting its value to a new instance of the type `EventEmitter<Todo>` and decorating it with the `@Output` decorator.

Passing inputs and consuming the outputs

Now, let's combine the components we defined in the preceding section and implement our complete application!

The last component we need to take a look at is `TodoApp`:

```
@Component({
  selector: 'todo-app',
  directives: [TodoList, InputBox],
  template: `
    <h1>Hello {{name}}!</h1>

    <p>
      Add a new todo:
      <input-box inputPlaceholder="New todo..."
        buttonLabel="Add"
        (inputText)="addTodo($event)">
      </input-box>
    </p>
```

```
<p>Here's the list of pending todo items:</p>
<todo-list [todos]="todos" (toggle)="toggleCompletion($event)"></
todo-list>
  `
})
class TodoApp {...}
```

Initially, we define the `TodoApp` class and decorate it with the `@Component` decorator. Note that in the list of the directives used by the component, we include `InputBox` and `TodoList`. The magic of how these components collaborate together happens in the template:

```
<input-box inputPlaceholder="New todo..."
  buttonLabel="Add"
  (inputText)="addTodo($event)">
</input-box>
```

First, we use the `InputBox` component and pass values to the inputs: `inputPlaceholder` and `buttonLabel`. Note that just like we saw earlier, if we want to pass an expression as a value to any of these inputs, we need to surround them with brackets (that is, `[inputPlaceholder]="expression"`). In this case, the expression will be evaluated in the context of the component that owns the template, and it will be passed as an input to the component that owns the given property.

Right after we pass the value for the `buttonLabel` input, we consume the `inputText` output by setting the value of the `(inputText)` attribute to the `addTodo($event)` expression. The value of `$event` will equal the value we passed to the `emit` method of the `inputText` object inside the `emitText` method of `InputBox` (in case we bind to a native event, the value of the event object will be the native event object itself).

In the same way, we pass the input of the `TodoList` component and handle its toggle output. Now, let's define the logic behind the `TodoApp` component:

```
class TodoApp {
  todos: Todo[] = [];
  name: string = 'John';
  addTodo(label: string) {
    this.todos.push({
      label,
      completed: false
    });
  }
  toggleCompletion(todo: Todo) {
    todo.completed = !todo.completed;
  }
}
```

In the `addTodo` method, we simply push a new to-do item to the `todos` array. The implementation of `toggleCompletion` is even simpler—we toggle the value of the completed flag that is passed as an argument to the to-do item. Now, we are familiar with the basics of the components' inputs and outputs!

Event bubbling

In Angular, we have the same bubbling behavior we have in the DOM. For instance, if we have the following template:

```
<input-box inputPlaceholder="New todo..."
  buttonLabel="Add"
  (click)="handleClick($event)"
  (inputText)="addTodo($event)">
</input-box>
```

The declaration of `input-box` looks like this:

```
<input #todoInput [placeholder]="inputPlaceholder">
<button (click)="emitText(todoInput.value);
                  todoInput.value = '';">
  {{buttonLabel}}
</button>
```

Once the user clicks on the button defined within the template of the `input-box` component, the `handleClick($event)` expression will be evaluated.

Further, the `target` property of the first argument of `handleClick` will be the button itself, but the `currentTarget` property will be the `input-box` element.

 Note that unlike native events, ones triggered by `EventEmitter` will not bubble.

Renaming the inputs and outputs of a directive

Now, we will explore how we can rename the directives' inputs and outputs! Let's suppose that we have the following definition of the `TodoList` component:

```
class TodoList {
  ...
  @Output() toggle = new EventEmitter<Todo>();
  toggle(index: number) {
    ...
  }
}
```

The output of the component is called `toggle`; the method that handles changes in the checkboxes responsible for toggling completion of the individual to-do items is called `toggle` as well. This code will not be compiled as in the `TodoList` controller, we have two identifiers named in the same way. We have two options here: we can either rename the method or the property. If we rename the property, this will change the name of the component's output as well. So, the following line of code will no longer work:

```
<todo-list [toggle]="foobar($event)"...></todo-list>
```

What we can do instead is rename the `toggle` property and explicitly set the name of the output using the `@Output` decorator:

```
class TodoList {
  ...
  @Output('toggle') toggleEvent = new EventEmitter<Todo>();
  toggle(index: number) {
    ...
  }
}
```

This way, we will be able to trigger the `toggle` output using the `toggleEvent` property.

> Note that such renames could be confusing and are not considered as best practices. For a complete set of best practices visit `https://angular.io/styleguide`.

Similarly, we can rename component's inputs using the following code snippet:

```
class TodoList {
  @Input('todos') todoList: Todo[];
  @Output('toggle') toggleEvent = new EventEmitter<Todo>();
  toggle(index: number) {
    ...
  }
}
```

Now, no matter that we renamed the input and output properties of `TodoList`, it still has the same public interface:

```
<todo-list [todos]="todos"
  (toggle)="toggleCompletion($event)">
</todo-list>
```

An alternative syntax to define inputs and outputs

The @Input and @Output decorators are syntax sugar for easier declaration of the directive's inputs and outputs. The original syntax for this purpose is as follows:

```
@Directive({
  outputs: ['outputName: outputAlias'],
  inputs: ['inputName: inputAlias']
})
class Dir {
  outputName = new EventEmitter();
}
```

Using @Input and @Output, the preceding syntax is equivalent to this:

```
@Directive(...)
class Dir {
  @Output('outputAlias') outputName = new EventEmitter();
  @Input('inputAlias') inputName;
}
```

Although both have the same semantics, according to the best practices, we should use the latter one because it is easier to read and understand.

Explaining Angular 2's content projection

Content projection is an important concept when developing user interfaces. It allows us to project pieces of content into different places of the user interface of our application. Web Components solve this problem with the content element. In AngularJS 1.x, it is implemented with the infamous transclusion.

Angular 2 is inspired by modern web standards, especially Web Components, which led to the adoption of some of the methods of content projection used there. In this section, we'll look at them in the context of Angular 2 using the ng-content directive.

Basic content projection in Angular 2

Let's suppose we're building a component called `fancy-button`. This component will use the standard HTML button element and add some extra behavior to it. Here is the definition of the `fancy-button` component:

```
@Component({
  selector: 'fancy-button',
  template: '<button>Click me</button>'
})
class FancyButton { … }
```

Inside of the `@Component` decorator, we set the inline template of the component together with its selector. Now, we can use the component with the following markup:

```
<fancy-button></fancy-button>
```

On the screen, we are going to see a standard HTML button that has a label with the content **Click me**. This is not a very flexible way to define reusable UI components. Most likely, the users of the fancy button will need to change the content of the label to something, depending on their application.

In AngularJS 1.x, we were able to achieve this result with `ng-transclude`:

```
// AngularJS 1.x example
app.directive('fancyButton', function () {
  return {
    restrict: 'E',
    transclude: true,
    template: '<button><ng-transclude></ng-transclude></button>'
  };
});
```

In Angular 2, we have the `ng-content` element:

```
// ch4/ts/ng-content/app.ts
@Component({
  selector: 'fancy-button',
  template: '<button><ng-content></ng-content></button>'
})
class FancyButton { /* Extra behavior */ }
```

Now, we can pass custom content to the fancy button by executing this:

```
<fancy-button>Click <i>me</i> now!</fancy-button>
```

As a result, the content between the opening and the closing `fancy-button` tags will be placed where the `ng-content` directive resides.

Projecting multiple content chunks

Another typical use case of content projection is when we pass content to a custom Angular 2 component or AngularJS 1.x directive and we want different parts of this content to be projected to different locations in the template.

For instance, let's suppose we have a `panel` component that has a title and a body:

```
<panel>
  <panel-title>Sample title</panel-title>
  <panel-content>Content</panel-content>
</panel>
```

And we have the following template of our component:

```
<div class="panel">
  <div class="panel-title">
    <!-- Project the content of panel-title here -->
  </div>
  <div class="panel-content">
    <!-- Project the content of panel-content here -->
  </div>
</div>`
```

In AngularJS 1.5, we are able to do this using multi-slot transclusion, which was implemented in order to allow us to have a smoother transition to Angular 2. Let's take a look at how we can proceed in Angular 2 in order to define such a `panel` component:

```
// ch4/ts/ng-content/app.ts
@Component({
  selector: 'panel',
  styles: [ ... ],
  template: `
    <div class="panel">
      <div class="panel-title">
        <ng-content select="panel-title"></ng-content>
      </div>
      <div class="panel-content">
```

```
            <ng-content select="panel-content"></ng-content>
        </div>
    </div>`
})
class Panel { }
```

We have already described the `selector` and `styles` properties, so let's take a look at the component's template. We have a `div` element with the `panel` class, which wraps the two nested `div` elements, respectively: one for the title of `panel` and one for the content of `panel`. In order to grab the content from the `panel-title` element and project it where the title of the `panel` is supposed to be in the rendered panel, we need to use the `ng-content` element with the `selector` attribute, which has the `panel-title` value. The value of the `selector` attribute is a CSS selector, which in this case is going to match all the `panel-title` elements that reside inside the target `panel` element. After this, `ng-content` will grab their content and set them as its own content.

Nesting components

We've already built a few simple applications as a composition of components and directives. We saw that components are basically directives with views, so we can implement them by nesting/composing other directives and components. The following figure illustrates this with a structural diagram:

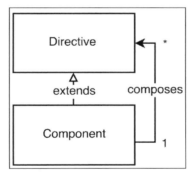

The composition could be achieved by nesting directives and components within the components' templates, taking advantage of the nested nature of the used markup. For instance, let's say we have a component with the `sample-component` selector, which has the following definition:

```
@Component({
    selector: 'sample-component',
    template: '<view-child></view-child>'
})
class Sample {}
```

The template of the `sample-component` selector has a single child element with the tag name `view-child`.

On the other hand, we can use the `sample-component` selector inside the template of another component, and since it can be used as an element, we can nest other components or directives inside it:

```
<sample-component>
  <content-child1></content-child1>
  <content-child2></content-child2>
</sample-component>
```

This way, the `sample-component` component has two different types of successors:

- The successor defined within its template.
- The successor that is passed as nested elements between its opening and closing tags.

In the context of Angular 2, the direct children elements defined within the component's template are called **view children** and the ones nested between its opening and closing tags are called **content children**.

Using ViewChildren and ContentChildren

Let's take a look at the implementation of the `Tabs` component, which uses the following structure:

```
<tabs (changed)="tabChanged($event)">
  <tab-title>Tab 1</tab-title>
  <tab-content>Content 1</tab-content>
  <tab-title>Tab 2</tab-title>
  <tab-content>Content 2</tab-content>
</tabs>
```

The preceding structure is composed of three components:

- The `Tab` component.
- The `TabTitle` component.
- The `TabContent` component.

Let's look at the implementation of the `TabTitle` component:

```
@Component({
  selector: 'tab-title',
  styles: [...],
```

```
  template: `
    <div class="tab-title" (click)="handleClick()">
      <ng-content></ng-content>
    </div>
  `
})
class TabTitle {
  tabSelected: EventEmitter<TabTitle> =
    new EventEmitter<TabTitle>();
  handleClick() {
    this.tabSelected.emit(this);
  }
}
```

There's nothing new in this implementation. We define a `TabTitle` component, which has a single property called `tabSelected`. It is of the type `EventEmitter` and will be triggered once the user clicks on the tab title.

Now, let's take a look at the `TabContent` component:

```
@Component({
  selector: 'tab-content',
  styles: [...],
  template: `
    <div class="tab-content" [hidden]="!isActive">
      <ng-content></ng-content>
    </div>
  `
})
class TabContent {
  isActive: boolean = false;
}
```

This has an even simpler implementation—all we do is project the DOM passed to the `tab-content` element inside `ng-content` and hide it once the value of the `isActive` property becomes `false`.

The interesting part of the implementation is the `Tabs` component itself:

```
// ch4/ts/basic-tab-content-children/app.ts
@Component({
  selector: 'tabs',
  styles: [...],
  template: `
    <div class="tab">
      <div class="tab-nav">
```

```
        <ng-content select="tab-title"></ng-content>
      </div>
      <ng-content select="tab-content"></ng-content>
    </div>
    `
})
class Tabs {
  @Output('changed')
  tabChanged: EventEmitter<number> = new EventEmitter<number>();

  @ContentChildren(TabTitle)
  tabTitles: QueryList<TabTitle>;

  @ContentChildren(TabContent)
  tabContents: QueryList<TabContent>;

  active: number;
  select(index: number) {…}
  ngAfterViewInit() {…}
}
```

In this implementation, we have a decorator that we haven't used yet—the
@ContentChildren decorator. The @ContentChildren property decorator fetches
the content children of the given component. This means that we can get references
to all TabTitle and TabContent instances from within the instance of the Tabs
component and get them in the order in which they are declared in the markup.
There's an alternative decorator called @ViewChildren, which fetches all the view
children of the given element. Let's take a look at the difference between them before
we explain the implementation further.

ViewChild versus ContentChild

Although both concepts sound similar, they have quite different semantics. In order
to understand them better, let's take a look at the following example:

```
// ch4/ts/view-child-content-child/app.ts
@Component({
  selector: 'user-badge',
  template: '…'
})
class UserBadge {}

@Component({
  selector: 'user-rating',
```

```
  template: '…'
})
class UserRating {}
```

Here, we've defined two components: `UserBadge` and `UserRating`. Let's define a parent component, which comprises both the components:

```
@Component({
  selector: 'user-panel',
  template: '<user-badge></user-badge>',
  directives: [UserBadge]
})
class UserPanel {…}
```

Note that the template of the view of `UserPanel` contains only the `UserBadge` component's selector. Now, let's use the `UserPanel` component in our application:

```
@Component({
  selector: 'app',
  template: `<user-panel>
    <user-rating></user-rating>
  </user-panel>`,
  directives: [CORE_DIRECTIVES, UserPanel, UserRating]
})
class App {
  constructor() {}
}
```

The template of our main `App` component uses the `UserPanel` component and nests the `UserRating` component inside it. Now, let's suppose we want to get a reference to the instance of the `UserRating` component that is used inside the `user-panel` element in the `App` component and a reference to the `UserBadge` component, which is used inside the `UserPanel` template. In order to do this, we can add two more properties to the `UserPanel` controller and add the `@ContentChild` and `@ViewChild` decorators to them with the appropriate arguments:

```
class UserPanel {
  @ViewChild(UserBadge)
  badge: UserBadge;

  @ContentChild(UserRating)
  rating: UserRating;
  constructor() {
    //
  }
}
```

The semantics of the badge property declaration is this: "get the instance of the first child component of the type UserBadge, which is used inside the UserPanel template". Accordingly, the semantics of the rating property's declaration is this: "get the instance of the first child component of the type UserRating, which is nested inside the UserPanel host element".

Now, if you run this code, you'll note that the values of the badge and rating properties are still equal to the undefined value inside the controller's constructor. This is because they are still not initialized in this phase of the component's life cycle. The life cycle hooks that we can use in order to get a reference to these child components are ngAfterViewInit and ngAfterContentInit. We can use these hooks simply by adding definitions of the ngAfterViewInit and ngAfterContentInit methods to the component's controller. We will make a complete overview of the life cycle hooks that Angular 2 provides shortly.

To recap, we can say that the content children of the given components are the child elements that are nested within the component's host element. In contrast, the view children directives of the given component are the elements used within its template.

 In order to get platform independent reference to a DOM element, again, we can use @ContentChildren and @ViewChildren. For instance, if we have the following template: <input #todo> we can get a reference to the input by using: @ViewChild('todo').

Since we are already familiar with the core differences between view children and content children now, we can continue with our tabs implementation.

In the tabs component, instead of using the @ContentChild decorator, we use @ContentChildren. We do this because we have multiple content children and we want to get them all:

```
@ContentChildren(TabTitle)
tabTitles: QueryList<TabTitle>;

@ContentChildren(TabContent)
tabContents: QueryList<TabContent>;
```

Another main difference we can notice is that the types of the tabTitles and tabContents properties are QueryList with the respective type parameter and not the component's type itself. We can think of the QueryList data structure as a JavaScript array—we can apply the same high-order functions (map, filter, reduce, and so on) over it and loop over its elements; however, QueryList is also observable, that is, we can observe it for changes.

As the final step of our `Tabs` definition, let's take a peek at the implementation of the `ngAfterContentInit` and select methods:

```
ngAfterContentInit() {
  this.tabTitles
    .map(t => t.tabSelected)
    .forEach((t, i) => {
      t.subscribe(_ => {
        this.select(i)
      });
    });
  this.active = 0;
  this.select(0);
}
```

In the first line of the method's implementation, we loop all `tabTitles` and take the observable's references. These objects have a method called `subscribe`, which accepts a callback as an argument. Once the `.emit()` method of the `EventEmitter` instance (that is, the `tabSelected` property of any tab) is called, the callback passed to the `subscribe` method will be invoked.

Now, let's take a look at the `select` method's implementation:

```
select(index: number) {
  let contents: TabContent[] = this.tabContents.toArray();
  contents[this.active].isActive = false;
  this.active = index;
  contents[this.active].isActive = true;
  this.tabChanged.emit(index);
}
```

In the first line, we get an array representation of `tabContents`, which is of the type `QueryList<TabContent>`. After that, we set the `isActive` flag of the current active tab to `false` and select the next active one. In the last line in the `select` method's implementation, we trigger the selected event of the `Tabs` component by invoking `this.tabChanged.emit` with the index of the currently selected tab.

Hooking into the component's life cycle

Components in Angular 2 have a well-defined life cycle, which allows us to hook into different phases of it and have further control over our application. We can do this by implementing specific methods in the component's controller. In order to be more explicit, thanks to the expressiveness of TypeScript, we can implement different interfaces associated with the life cycle's phases. Each of these interfaces has a single method, which is associated with the phase itself.

Although code written with explicit interface implementation will have better semantics, since Angular 2 supports ES5 as well within the component, we can simply define methods with the same names as the life cycle hooks (but this time, prefixed with ng) and take advantage of duck typing.

The following diagram shows all the phases we can hook into:

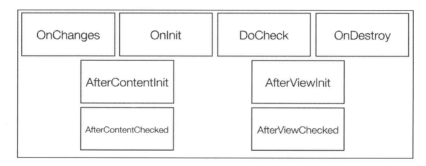

Let's take a look at the different life cycle hooks:

- OnChanges: This hook will be invoked once a change in the input properties of a given component has been detected. For instance, let's take a look at the following component:

```
@Component({
  selector: 'panel',
  inputs: ['title']
})
class Panel {...}
```

We can use it like this:

```
<panel [title]="expression"></panel>
```

Once the value of the expression associated with the [title] attribute has been changed, the ngOnChanges hook will be invoked. We can implement it using this code snippet:

```
@Component (...)
class Panel {
  ngOnChanges(changes) {
    Object.keys(changes).forEach(prop => {
      console.log(prop, 'changed. Previous value', changes[prop].
previousValue);
    });
  }
}
```

The preceding snippet will display all the changed bindings and their old values. In order to be more explicit in the implementation of the hook, we can use interfaces:

```
import {Component, OnChanges} from '@angular/core';
@Component (...)
class Panel implements OnChanges {
  ngOnChanges(changes) {...}
}
```

All the interfaces representing the individual life cycle hooks define a single method with the name of the interface itself prefixed with ng. In the upcoming list, we'll use the term life cycle hook, both for interface and/or the method, except if we won't imply anything specifically for only one of them.

- OnInit: This hook will be invoked once the given component has been initialized. We can implement it using the OnInit interface with its ngOnInit method.

- DoCheck: This will be invoked when the change detector of the given component is invoked. It allows us to implement our own change detection algorithm for the given component. Note that DoCheck and OnChanges should not be implemented together on the same directive.

- OnDestroy: If we implement the OnDestroy interface with its single ngOnDestroy method, we can hook into the destroy life cycle phase of a component. This method will be invoked once the component is detached from the component tree.

Now, let's take a look at the life cycle hooks associated with the component's content and view children:

- `AfterContentInit`: If we implement the `ngAfterContentInit` life cycle hook, we will be notified when the component's content has been fully initialized. This is the phase when the properties decorated with `ContentChild` or `ContentChildren` will be initialized.

- `AfterContentChecked`: By implementing this hook, we'll get notified each time the content of the given component has been checked by the change detection mechanism of Angular 2.

- `AfterViewInit`: If we implement the `ngAfterViewInit` life cycle hook, we will be notified when the component's view has been fully initialized. This is the phase when the properties decorated with `ViewChild` or `ViewChildren` will be initialized.

- `AfterViewChecked`: This is similar to `AfterContentChecked`. The `AfterViewChecked` hook will be invoked once the view of your component has been checked.

The order of execution

In order to trace the order of execution of the callbacks associated with each hook, let's take a peek at the `ch4/ts/life-cycle/app.ts` example:

```
@Component({
  selector: 'panel',
  inputs: ['title', 'caption'],
  template: '<ng-content></ng-content>'
})
class Panel {
  ngOnChanges(changes) {…}
  ngOnInit() {…}
  ngDoCheck() {…}
  ngOnDestroy() {…}
  ngAfterContentInit() {…}
  ngAfterContentChecked() {…}
  ngAfterViewInit() {…}
  ngAfterViewChecked() {…}
}
```

The `Panel` component implements all the hooks without explicitly implementing the interfaces associated with them.

We can use the component in the following template:

```
<button (click)="toggle()">Toggle</button>
<div *ngIf="counter % 2 == 0">
  <panel caption="Sample caption" title="Sample">Hello world!</panel>
</div>
```

In the preceding example, we have a panel and a button. Upon each click on the button, the panel will be either removed or appended to the view by the ngIf directive.

During the application initialization, if the result of the "counter % 2 == 0" expression is evaluated to true, the ngOnChanges method will be invoked. This happens because the values of the title and caption properties are going to be set for the first time.

Right after this, the ngOnInit method will be called, since the component has been initialized. Once the component's initialization is completed, the change detection will be triggered, which will lead to the invocation of the ngDoCheck method that allows us to hook custom logic for detecting changes in the state.

 Note that you are not supposed to implement both ngDoCheck and ngOnChanges methods for the same component, since they are mutually exclusive. The example here does this for learning purposes only.

After the ngDoCheck method, the component's content will be followed by performing a check on it (ngAfterContentInit and ngAfterContentChecked will be invoked in this order). Right after this, the same will happen for the component's view (ngAfterViewInit followed by ngAfterViewChecked).

Once the expression of the ngIf directive is evaluated to false, the entire component will be detached from the view, which will lead to the invocation of the ngOnDestroy hook.

On the next button click, if the value of the expression of ngIf is equal to true, the same sequence of calls of the life cycle hooks as the one during the initialization phase will be executed.

Defining generic views with TemplateRef

We are already familiar with the concepts of inputs, content, and view children, and we also know when we can get a reference to them in the component's life cycle. Now, we will combine them and introduce a new concept: TemplateRef.

Let's take a step back and take a look at the last to-do application we developed earlier in this chapter. In the following screenshot, you can see what its UI looks like:

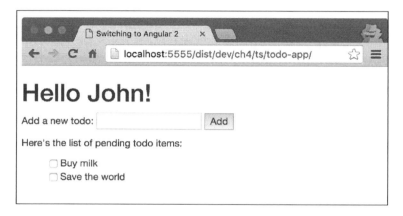

If we take a look at its implementation in ch4/ts/inputs-outputs/app.ts, we'll see that the template used to render the individual to-do items is defined inside the template of the entire to-do application.

What if we want to use a different layout to render the to-do items? We can do this by creating another component called Todo, which encapsulates the responsibility of rendering them. Then, we can define separate Todo components for the different layouts we want to support. This way, we need to have *n* different components for *n* different layouts, even though we use only their templates.

Angular 2 comes with a more elegant solution. Earlier in this chapter, we already discussed the template element. We said that it allows us to define a chunk of HTML that will not be processed by the browser. Angular 2 allows us to reference such template elements and use them by passing them as content children!

Here is how we can pass the custom layout to our refactored `todo-app` component:

```
// ch4/ts/template-ref/app.ts
<todo-app>
  <template let-todo>
    <input type="checkbox" [checked]="todo.completed"
      (change)="todo.completed = !todo.completed;">
    <span [class.completed]="todo.completed">
      {{todo.label}}
    </span><br>
  </template>
</todo-app>
```

In the template, we declare a variable called `todo`. Later in the template, we can use it to specify the way in which we want to visualize the content.

Now, let's see how we can get a reference to this template in the controller of the `TodoApp` component:

```
// ch4/ts/template-ref/app.ts
class TodoApp {
  @ContentChild(TemplateRef)
  private itemsTemplate: TemplateRef;
  // ...
}
```

All we do here is define a property called `itemsTemplate` and decorate it with the `@ContentChild` decorator. During the component's life cycle (more accurately, in `ngAfterContentInit`), the value of `itemsTemplate` will be set as a reference of the template that we passed as the content of the `todo-app` element.

There is one more problem though—we need the template in the `TodoList` component, since that's the place where we render the individual to-do items. What we can do is define another input of the `TodoList` component and pass the template directly from `TodoApp`:

```
// ch4/ts/template-ref/app.ts
class TodoList {
  @Input() todos: Todo[];
  @Input() itemsTemplate: TemplateRef;
  @Output() toggle = new EventEmitter<Todo>();
}
```

We need to pass it as an input from the template of `TodoApp`:

```
...
<todo-list [todos]="todos"
  [itemsTemplate]="itemsTemplate">
</todo-list>
```

The only thing left is to use this template reference in the template of the `TodoList` application:

```
<!-- … -->
<template *ngFor="let todo of todos; template: itemsTemplate"></template>
```

We explained the extended syntax of the `ngForOf` directive in the previous sections of this chapter. This snippet shows one more property of this directive that we can set: the `ngForTemplate` property. By default, the template of the `ngForOf` directive is the element it is used on. By specifying a template reference to the `ngForTemplate` property, we can use the passed `TemplateRef` instead.

Understanding and enhancing the change detection

We already briefly described the change detection mechanism of the framework. We said that compared to AngularJS 1.x, where it runs in the context of the scope, in Angular 2, it runs in the context of the individual components. Another concept we mentioned is the zones, which basically intercept all the asynchronous calls that we can make using the browser APIs and provide execution context for the change detection mechanism of the framework. Zones fix the annoying problem we have in AngularJS 1.x, where when we use APIs outside of Angular, we need to explicitly invoke the `digest` loop.

In *Chapters 1, Getting Started with Angular 2* and *Chapter 2, The Building Blocks of an Angular 2 Application*, we discussed that there are two main implementations of the change detector: `DynamicChangeDetector` and `JitChangeDetector`. The first one works great for environments with strict **CSP (Content-Security-Policy)** because of the disabled dynamic evaluation of JavaScript. The second one takes great benefits from the inline-caching mechanism of the JavaScript virtual machine and therefore brings great performance!

In this section, we'll explore another property of the @Component decorator's configuration object, which provides us further control over the change detection mechanism of the framework by changing its strategy. By explicitly setting the strategy, we are able to prevent the change detection mechanism from running over a component's subtrees, which in some cases can bring great performance benefits.

The order of execution of the change detectors

Now, let's briefly describe the order in which the change detectors are invoked in a given component tree.

For this purpose, we will use the last implementation of the to-do application we have, but this time, we'll extract the logic to render the individual to-do items into a separate component called TodoItem. In the following figure, we can see the application's structure:

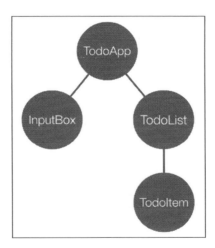

At the top level is the TodoApp component, which has two children: InputBox and TodoList. The TodoList component renders the individual to-do items in TodoItem components. The implementation details are not important for our purpose, so we are going to ignore them.

Now, we need to realize that there is an implicit dependency between the state of the parent component and its children. For instance, the state of the TodoList component depends completely on the to-do items that are located at its parent: the TodoApp component. There's a similar dependency between TodoItem and TodoList, since the TodoList component passes the individual to-do items to a separate instance of the TodoItem component.

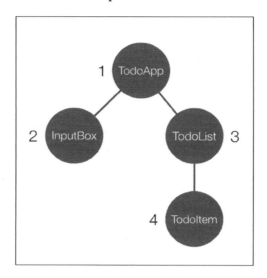

Because of our last observation, the order of execution of the change detectors attached to the individual components is like the one shown on the preceding figure. Once the change detection mechanism run, initially it will perform a check over the TodoApp component. Right after this, the InputBox component will be checked for changes, followed by the TodoList component. In the end, Angular will invoke the change detector of the TodoItem component.

You can trace the order of execution in the ch4/ts/change_detection_strategy_ order/app.ts example, where each individual component logs a message once its ngDoCheck method is invoked.

 Note that only the components have an instance of a change detector attached to them; directives use the change detector of their parent component.

Change detection strategies

The change detection strategies that Angular 2 provides are: `Default` and `OnPush`. We will describe how we can take advantage of `OnPush` in detail, since it is very powerful when working with immutable data. Before taking a deep dive into `OnPush`, lets briefly describe what impact the change detection strategy can have on our application.

Now, let's import the TypeScript `enum`, which can be used to configure the strategy used for the individual components:

```
// ch4/ts/change_detection_strategy_broken/app.ts
import {ChangeDetectionStrategy} from '@angular/core';
```

We can configure the `TodoList` component to use the `OnPush` strategy:

```
@Component({
  selector: 'todo-list',
  changeDetection: ChangeDetectionStrategy.OnPush,
  template: `...`,
  styles: [...]
})
class TodoList { … }
```

This way, the change detection will be skipped until the `TodoList` component gets an object with different reference as input. But what does it mean to prevent the change detection from running? You can go to `http://localhost:5555/dist/dev/ch4/ts/change_detection_strategy_broken/` and see the inconsistent behavior of the `TodoList` component. When you add a new to-do item in the input and you click on the button, it won't immediately appear in the list.

Performance boosting with immutable data and OnPush

In this section we're going to describe the `OnPush` change detection strategy. It is extremely useful when the result that the given component produces depends only on its inputs. In such cases, we can pass immutable data to the inputs in order to make sure that it will not be mutated by any other component. This way, by having a component that depends only on its immutable inputs, we can make sure that it produces different user interfaces only once it receives different inputs (that is, different reference).

In this section, we are going to apply the OnPush strategy on the TodoList component. Since it depends only on its inputs (the todos input), we want to make sure that its change detection will be performed only once it receives a new reference of the todos collection.

The essence of immutable data is that it cannot change. This means that once we add a new to-do item to the todos collection, we cannot change it; instead, the add (or in our case, push) method will return a new collection—a copy of the initial collection with the new item included.

This may seem like a huge overhead—to copy the entire collection on each change. In big applications, this may have a big performance impact. However, we don't need to copy the entire collection. There are libraries that implement immutable data structure using smarter algorithms: persistent data structures. Persistent data structures are out of the scope of the current content. Further information about them can be found in most computer science textbooks for advanced data structures. The good thing is that we don't have to understand their implementation in depth in order to use them! There is a library called Immutable.js that implements a few commonly used immutable data structures. In our case, we are going to use the immutable list. Generally, the immutable list behaves just like a normal list, but on each operation that is supposed to mutate it, it returns a new list.

This means that if we have a list called foo, which is immutable, and we append a new item to the list, we are going to get a new reference:

```
let foo = List.of(1, 2, 3);
let changed = foo.push(4);
foo === changed // false
console.log(foo.toJS()); // [ 1, 2, 3 ]
console.log(changed.toJS()); // [ 1, 2, 3, 4 ]
```

In order to take advantage of immutability, we need to install Immutable.js using npm.

We've already done this in ch4/ts/change_detection_strategy/app.ts. Immutable.js is already part of package.json, which is located at the root directory of the project.

Now, it's time to refactor our to-do application and make it use immutable data!

Using immutable data structures in Angular

Let's take a look at how we currently keep the to-do items in the `TodoApp` component:

```
class TodoApp {
  todos: Todo[] = [...];
  ...
}
```

We use an array of `Todo` items. The JavaScript array is mutable, which means that if we pass it to a component that uses the `OnPush` strategy, it is not safe to skip the change detection in case we get the same input reference. For instance, we may have two components that use the same list of to-do items. Both components can modify the list since it is mutable. This will lead to an inconsistent state to any of the components in case their change detection is not performed. That's why we need to make sure that the list that holds the items is immutable. All we need to do in the `TodoApp` component in order to make sure that it holds its data in an immutable data structure is this:

```
// ch4/ts/change_detection_strategy/app.ts
class TodoApp {
  todos: ImmutableList<Todo> = ImmutableList.of({
    label: 'Buy milk',
    completed: false
  }, {
    label: 'Save the world',
    completed: false
  });
  ...
}
```

In this way, we construct the `todos` property as an immutable list. Since the mutation operations of the immutable list return a new list, we need to make a slight modification in `addTodo` and `toggleTodoCompletion`:

```
...
addTodo(label: string) {
  this.todos = this.todos.push({
    label,
    completed: false
  });
}
toggleCompletion(index: number) {
  this.todos = this.todos.update(index, todo => {
    let newTodo = {
```

```
      label: todo.label,
      completed: !todo.completed
    };
    return newTodo;
  });
}
...
```

The `addTodo` function looks exactly the same as before except that we set the result of the `push` method as a value to the `todos` property.

In `toggleTodoCompletion`, we use the `update` method of the immutable list. As the first argument, we pass the index of the to-do item we want to modify, and the second argument is a callback that does the actual modification. Note that since we are using immutable data in this case, we copy the modified to-do item. This is required because it tells the `update` method that the item with the given index has been changed (since it is immutable, it is considered as changed only when it has a new reference), which means that the entire list has been changed.

That was the complex part! Now let's take a look at the `TodoList` component's definition:

```
@Component({
  selector: 'todo-list',
  changeDetection: ChangeDetectionStrategy.OnPush,
  template: `...`,
  styles: [...]
})
class TodoList {
  @Input() todos: ImmutableList<Todo>;
  @Output() toggle = new EventEmitter<number>();
  toggleCompletion(index: number) {
    this.toggle.emit(index);
  }
}
```

Inside the `@Component` decorator, we set the `changeDetection` property to the value of the `OnPush` strategy. This means that the component will run its change detector only when any of its inputs gets a new reference. The template of the component stays exactly the same since `ngForOf` internally uses ES2015 iterators to loop the items in the provided collection. They are supported by `Immutable.js`, so the changes in the template are not required.

Since we need the index of the changed item (the one we use in the `update` method of the `todos` collection in `TodoApp`), we change the type of the output of the component to `EventEmitter<number>`. In `toggleCompletion`, we emit the index of the changed to-do item.

This is how we optimized our simple to-do application by preventing the change detection mechanism from running in the entire right subtree in case the parent component hasn't pushed an input with a new reference.

Summary

In this chapter, we went through the core building blocks of an Angular 2 application: directives and components. We built a couple of sample components, which show us the syntax to be used for the definition of these fundamental concepts. We also described the life cycle of each directive and the core set of features the given directive and component have. As the next step, we saw how we can enhance the performance of our application by using the `OnPush` change detection strategy with immutable data.

The next chapter is completely dedicated to the Angular 2 services and the dependency injection mechanism of the framework. We are going to look at how we can define and instantiate custom injectors and how we can take advantage of the dependency injection mechanism in our directives and components.

5
Dependency Injection in Angular 2

In this chapter, we'll explain how to take advantage of the **dependency injection (DI)** mechanism of the framework with all its various features.

We will explore the following topics:

- Configuring and creating injectors.

- Instantiating objects using injectors.

- Injecting dependencies into our directives and components. This way, we will be able to reuse the business logic defined within the services and wire it up with the UI logic.

- Annotating the ES5 code we will write in order to get the exact same result we get when we are using the TypeScript syntax.

Why do I need Dependency Injection?

Let's suppose that we have a `Car` class that depends on the `Engine` and `Transmission` classes. How can we implement this system? Let's take a look:

```
class Engine {…}
class Transmission {…}
class Car {
  engine;
  transmission;
  constructor() {
    this.engine = new Engine();
    this.transmission = new Transmission();
  }
}
```

In this example, we created the dependencies of the Car class inside of its constructor. Although it looks simple, it is far from being flexible. Each time we create an instance of the Car class, instances of the same Engine and Transmission classes will be created. This may be problematic because of the following reasons:

- The Car class gets less testable because we can't test it independently from its engine and transmission dependencies.
- We couple the Car class with the logic used for the instantiation of its dependencies.

Dependency Injection in Angular 2

Another way we can approach this is by taking advantage of the DI pattern. We're already familiar with it from AngularJS 1.x. Let's demonstrate how we can refactor the preceding code using DI in the context of Angular 2:

```
class Engine {…}
class Transmission {…}

@Injectable()
class Car {
  engine;
  transmission;
  constructor(engine: Engine, transmission: Transmission) {
    this.engine = engine;
    this.transmission = transmission;
  }
}
```

All we did in the preceding snippet was add the @Injectable class decorator on top of the definition of the Car class and provide type annotations for the parameters of its constructor.

Benefits of DI in Angular 2

There is one more step left, which we'll take a look at in the next section. But let's see what the benefits of the mentioned approach are:

- We can easily pass different versions of the dependencies of the Car class for a testing environment.
- We're not coupled with the logic around the dependencies' instantiation.

The Car class is only responsible for implementing its own domain-specific logic instead of being coupled with additional functionalities, such as the management of its dependencies. Our code also got more declarative and easier to read.

Now, after we've realized some of the benefits of the DI, let's take a look at the missing pieces in order to make this code work!

Configuring an injector

The primitive used for the instantiation of the individual dependencies in our Angular 2 applications via the DI mechanism of the framework is called the **injector**. The injector contains a set of **providers** that encapsulate the logic for the instantiation of registered dependencies associated with **tokens**. We can think of tokens as identifiers of the different providers registered within the injector.

Let's take a look at the following snippet, which is located at ch5/ts/injector-basics/injector.ts:

```
import 'reflect-metadata';
import {
  ReflectiveInjector, Inject, Injectable,
  OpaqueToken
} from '@angular/core';

const BUFFER_SIZE = new OpaqueToken('buffer-size');

class Buffer {
  constructor(@Inject(BUFFER_SIZE) private size: Number) {
    console.log(this.size);
  }
}

@Injectable()
class Socket {
  constructor(private buffer: Buffer) {}
}

let injector = ReflectiveInjector.resolveAndCreate([
  { provide: BUFFER_SIZE, useValue: 42 },
  Buffer,
  Socket
]);

injector.get(Socket);
```

You can run the file using the following command:

```
cd app
ts-node ch5/ts/injector-basics/injector.ts
```

If you haven't installed `ts-node` yet, take a look at *Chapter 3, TypeScript Crash Course*, which explains how you can proceed in order to have it up and running on your computer.

We import `ReflectiveInjector`, `Injectable`, `Inject`, and `OpaqueToken`.

Injector represents the **container** used for the instantiation of the different dependencies, respectively the `ReflectiveInjector` is a concrete class which implements this abstraction. Using the rules declared with providers and the metadata generated by the TypeScript compiler, it knows how to create them.

In the preceding snippet, we initially defined the `BUFFER_SIZE` constant and set it to the `new OpaqueToken('buffer-size')` value. We can think of the value of `BUFFER_SIZE` as a unique value that cannot be duplicated in the application (`OpaqueToken` is an alternative of the `Symbol` class from ES2015, since at the time of writing this, it is not supported by TypeScript).

We defined two classes: `Buffer` and `Socket`. The `Buffer` class has a constructor that accepts only a single dependency called `size`, which is of the type `Number`. In order to add additional metadata for the process of dependency resolution, we use the `@Inject` parameter decorator. This decorator accepts an identifier (also known as **token**) of the dependency we want to inject. Usually, it is the type of the dependency (that is, a reference of a class), but in some cases, it can be a different type of a value. For example, in our case, we used the instance of the `OpaqueToken` class.

Dependency resolution with generated metadata

Now let's take a look at the `Socket` class. We decorate it with the `@Injectable` decorator. This decorator is supposed to be used by any class that accepts dependencies that should be injected via the dependency injection mechanism of Angular 2.

The `@Injectable` decorator forces the TypeScript compiler to generate additional metadata for the types of dependencies that a given class accepts. This means that if we omit the `@Injectable` decorator, Angular's DI mechanism will not be aware of the tokens associated with the dependencies it needs to resolve.

TypeScript doesn't generate any metadata if no decorator is used on top of a class mostly for performance concerns. Imagine if such metadata was generated for each individual class that accepts dependencies—in this case, the output would be bloated with additional type metadata that would be unused.

An alternative to using @Injectable is to explicitly declare the types of dependencies using the @Inject decorator. Take a look at the following:

```
class Socket {
  constructor(@Inject(Buffer) private buffer: Buffer) {}
}
```

This means that the preceding code has equivalent semantics to the code that uses @Injectable, as mentioned earlier. The only difference is that Angular 2 will get the type of dependency (that is, the token associated with it) explicitly (directly from the metadata added by the @Injector decorator) compared to the case where @Injectable is used, when it will look at the metadata generated by the compiler.

Instantiating an injector

Now, let's create an instance of an injector in order to use it for the instantiation of registered tokens:

```
let injector = ReflectiveInjector.resolveAndCreate([
  { provide: BUFFER_SIZE, useValue: 42 },
  Buffer,
  Socket
]);
```

We create an instance of the ReflectiveInjector using its static method called resolveAndCreate. This is a factory method that accepts an array of providers as argument and returns a new ReflectiveInjector.

resolve means that the providers will go through a resolution process, which includes some internal processing (flattening multiple nested arrays and converting individual providers into an array). Later, the injector can instantiate any of the dependencies for which we have registered providers based on the rules the providers encapsulate.

In our case, we used the provider declaration in order to explicitly tell the Angular 2 DI mechanism to use the value 42 when the BUFFER_SIZE token is required. The other two providers are implicit. Angular 2 will instantiate them by invoking the provided class with the new operator once all of their dependencies are resolved.

We request the `BUFFER_SIZE` value in the constructor of the `Buffer` class:

```
class Buffer {
  constructor(@Inject(BUFFER_SIZE) private size: Number) {
    console.log(this.size);
  }
}
```

In the preceding example, we used the `@Inject` parameter decorator. It hints the DI mechanism that the first argument of the constructor of the `Buffer` class should be instantiated with the provider associated with the `BUFFER_SIZE` token passed to the injector.

Introducing forward references

Angular 2 introduced the concept of **forward references**. It is required due to the following reasons:

- ES2015 classes are not hoisted.
- Allow resolution of the dependencies that are declared after the declaration of the dependent providers.

In this section, we're going to explain the problem that forward references solve and the way we can take advantage of them.

Now, let's suppose that we have defined the `Buffer` and `Socket` classes in the opposite order:

```
// ch5/ts/injector-basics/forward-ref.ts

@Injectable()
class Socket {
  constructor(private buffer: Buffer) {…}
}

// undefined
console.log(Buffer);

class Buffer {
  constructor(@Inject(BUFFER_SIZE) private size: Number) {…}
}

// [Function: Buffer]
console.log(Buffer);
```

Here, we have the exact same dependencies as in the ones in the previous example, but in this case, the `Socket` class definition precedes the definition of the `Buffer` class. Note that the value of the `Buffer` identifier will equal `undefined` until the JavaScript virtual machine evaluates the declaration of the `Buffer` class. However, the metadata for the types of dependencies that `Socket` accepts will be generated and placed right after the `Socket` class definition. This means that along with the interpretation of the generated JavaScript, the value of the `Buffer` token will equal `undefined`—that is, as a type of dependency (or in the context of the DI mechanism of Angular 2, its token), the framework will get an invalid value.

Running the preceding snippet will result in a runtime error of the following form:

```
Error: Cannot resolve all parameters for Socket(undefined). Make sure
they all have valid type or annotations.
```

The best way to resolve this issue is by swapping the definitions with their proper order. Another way we can proceed is to take advantage of a solution that Angular 2 provides: a forward reference:

```
...
import {forwardRef} from '@angular/core';
...
@Injectable()
class Socket {
  constructor(@Inject(forwardRef(() => Buffer))
    private buffer: Buffer) {}
}
class Buffer {...}
```

The preceding snippet demonstrates how we can take advantage of forward references. All we need to do is use the `@Inject` parameter decorator and pass the result of the invocation of the `forwardRef` function to it. The `forwardRef` function is a higher-order function that accepts a single argument—another function that is responsible for returning the token associated with the dependency (or more precisely associated with its provider) that needs to be injected. This way, the framework provides a way to defer the process of resolving the types (tokens) of dependencies.

The token of the dependency will be resolved the first time `Socket` needs to be instantiated, unlike the default behavior in which the token is required at the time of the declaration of the given class.

Configuring providers

Now, let's take a look at an example similar to the one used earlier but with a different configuration of the injector:

```
let injector = ReflectiveInjector.resolveAndCreate([
{ provide: BUFFER_SIZE, useValue: 42 },
{ provide: Buffer, useClass: Buffer },
{ provide: Socket, useClass: Socket }
]);
```

In this case, inside of the provider, we explicitly declared that we want the Buffer class to be used for the construction of the dependency with a token equal to the reference of the Buffer class. We do the exact same thing for the dependency associated with the Socket token; but this time, we provide the Socket class instead. This is how Angular 2 will proceed when we omit the explicit provider definition and pass only a reference to a class instead.

Explicitly declaring the class used for the instantiation of the same class may seem quite worthless, and given the examples we looked at so far, this'll be completely correct. In some cases, however, we might want to provide a different class for the instantiation of a dependency associated with given class token.

For instance, let's suppose we have the Http service that is used in a service called UserService:

```
class Http {...}

@Injectable()
class UserService {
  constructor(private http: Http) {}
}

let injector = ReflectiveInjector.resolveAndCreate([
  UserService,
  Http
]);
```

The `UserService` service uses `Http` for communication with a RESTful service. We can instantiate `UserService` using `injector.get(UserService)`. This way, the constructor of `UserService` invoked by the injector's `get` method will accept an instance of the `Http` service as an argument. However, if we want to test `UserService`, we don't really need to make HTTP calls to the RESTful service. In case of unit testing, we can provide a dummy implementation that will only fake these HTTP calls. In order to inject an instance of a different class to the `UserService` service, we can change the configuration of the injector to the following:

```
class DummyHttp {...}

// ...

let injector = ReflectiveInjector.resolveAndCreate([
  UserService,
  { provide: Http, useClass: DummyHttp }
]);
```

Now, when we instantiate `UserService`, it's constructor will receive a reference to an instance of the `DummyHttp` service. This code is available at `ch5/ts/configuring-providers/dummy-http.ts`.

Using existing providers

Another way to proceed is using the `useExisting` property of the provider's configuration object:

```
// ch5/ts/configuring-providers/existing.ts
let injector = ReflectiveInjector.resolveAndCreate([
  DummyService,
  { provide: Http, useExisting: DummyService },
  UserService
]);
```

In the preceding snippet, we registered three tokens: `DummyService`, `UserService`, and `Http`. We declared that we want to bind the `Http` token to the existing token, `DummyService`. This means that when the `Http` service is requested, the injector will find the provider for the token used as the value of the `useExisting` property and instantiate it or get the value associated with it. We can think of `useExisting` as creating an alias of the given token:

```
let dummyHttp = {
  get() {},
  post() {}
};
```

```
let injector = ReflectiveInjector.resolveAndCreate([
  { provide: DummyService, useValue: dummyHttp },
  { provide: Http, useExisting: DummyService },
  UserService
]);
console.assert(injector.get(UserService).http === dummyHttp);
```

The preceding snippet will create an alias of the `Http` token to the `DummyHttp` token. This means that once the `Http` token is requested, the call will be forwarded to the provider associated with the `DummyHttp` token, which will be resolved to the value `dummyHttp`.

Defining factories for instantiating services

Now, let's suppose we want to create a complex object, for example, one that represents a **Transport Layer Security (TLS)** connection. A few of the properties of such an object are a socket, a set of crypto protocols, and a certificate. In the context of this problem, the features of the DI mechanism of Angular 2 we have so far looked at might seem a bit limited.

For example, we might need to configure some of the properties of the `TLSConnection` class without coupling the process of its instantiation with all the configuration details (choose appropriate crypto algorithms, open the TCP socket over which we will establish the secure connection, and so on).

In this case, we can take advantage of the `useFactory` property of the provider's configuration object:

```
let injector = ReflectiveInjector.resolveAndCreate([
  { provide: TLSConnection,
    useFactory: (socket: Socket, certificate: Certificate, crypto:
Crypto) => {
      let connection = new TLSConnection();
      connection.certificate = certificate;
      connection.socket = socket;
      connection.crypto = crypto;
      socket.open();
      return connection;
    },
```

```
      deps: [Socket, Certificate, Crypto]
    }
    { provide: BUFFER_SIZE, useValue: 42 },
    Buffer,
    Socket,
    Certificate,
    Crypto
  ]);
```

The preceding code seems a bit complex at first, but let's take a look at it step by step. We can start with the parts we're already familiar with:

```
let injector = ReflectiveInjector.resolveAndCreate([
    ...
    { provide: BUFFER_SIZE, useValue: 42 },
    Buffer,
    Socket,
    Certificate,
    Crypto
  ]);
```

Initially, we registered a number of providers: Buffer, Socket, Certificate, and Crypto. Just like in the preceding example, we also registered the BUFFER_SIZE token and associated it with the value 42. This means that we can already create objects of the Buffer, Socket, Certificate, and Crypto types:

```
// buffer with size 42
console.log(injector.get(Buffer));
// socket with buffer with size 42
console.log(injector.get(Socket));
```

We can create and configure an instance of the TLSConnection object in the following way:

```
let connection = new TLSConnection();
connection.certificate = certificate;
connection.socket = socket;
connection.crypto = crypto;
socket.open();
return connection;
```

Now, if we register a provider that has the `TLSConnection` token as a dependency, we will prevent the dependency injection mechanism of Angular from taking care of the dependency resolution process. In order to handle this problem, we can use the `useFactory` property of the provider's configuration object. This way, we can specify a function in which we can manually create the instance of the object associated with the provider's token. We can use the `useFactory` property together with the `deps` property in order to specify the dependencies to be passed to the factory:

```
{ provide: TLSConnection,
  useFactory: (socket: Socket, certificate: Certificate, crypto:
Crypto) => {
    // ...
  },
  deps: [Socket, Certificate, Crypto]
}
```

In the preceding snippet, we defined the factory function used for the instantiation of `TLSConnection`. As dependencies, we declared `Socket`, `Certificate`, and `Crypto`. These dependencies are resolved by the DI mechanism of Angular 2 and injected to the factory function. You can take a look at the entire implementation and play with it at `ch5/ts/configuring-providers/factory.ts`.

Child injectors and visibility

In this section, we're going to take a look at how we can build a hierarchy of injectors. This is a completely new concept introduced by Angular 2. Each injector can have zero or one parent injectors and each parent injector can have zero or more children, respectively. In contrast to AngularJS 1.x, where all the registered providers are stored in a flat structure in Angular 2, they are stored in a tree. The flat structure is more limited; for instance, it doesn't support the namespacing of tokens; that is, we cannot declare different providers for the same token, which might be required in some cases. So far, we looked at an example of injector that doesn't have any children or a parent. Now let's build a hierarchy of injectors!

In order to gain a better understanding of this hierarchical structure of injectors, let's take a look at the following figure:

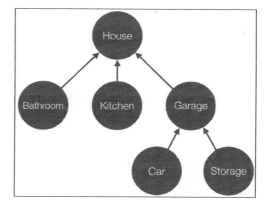

Here, we see a tree where each node is an injector and each of these injectors keeps a reference to its parent. Injector **House** has three child injectors: **Bathroom**, **Kitchen**, and **Garage**.

Garage has two children: **Car** and **Storage**. We can think of these injectors as containers with registered providers inside of them.

Let's suppose we want to get the value of the provider associated with the token **Tire**. If we use the injector **Car**, this means that Angular 2's DI mechanism will try to find the provider associated with this token in **Car** and all of its parents, **Garage** and **House**, until it finds it.

Building a hierarchy of injectors

In order to gain a better understanding of the previous paragraph, let's take a look at this simple example:

```
// ch5/ts/parent-child/simple-example.ts
class Http {}

@Injectable()
class UserService {
  constructor(public http: Http) {}
}

let parentInjector = ReflectiveInjector.resolveAndCreate([
  Http
]);
```

```
let childInjector = parentInjector.resolveAndCreateChild([
  UserService
]);

// UserService { http: Http {} }
console.log(childInjector.get(UserService));
// true
console.log(childInjector.get(Http) === parentInjector.get(Http));
```

The imports are omitted, since they are not essential to explain the preceding snippet. We have two services, Http and UserService, where UserService depends on the Http service.

Initially, we created an injector using the resolveAndCreate static method of the ReflectiveInjector class. We passed an implicit provider to this injector, which will later be resolved to a provider with an Http token. Using resolveAndCreateChild, we resolved the passed providers and instantiated an injector, which points to parentInjector (so we get the same relation as the one between **Garage** and **House** on the diagram above).

Now, using childInjector.get(UserService), we are able to get the value associated with the UserService token. Similarly, using childInjector.get(Http) and parentInjector.get(Http), we get the same value associated with the Http token. This means that childInjector asks its parent for the value associated with the requested token.

However, if we try to use parentInjector.get(UserService), we won't be able to get the value associated with the token, since in this injector, we don't have a registered provider with this token.

Configuring dependencies

Now that we're familiar with the injectors' hierarchy, let's see how we can get the dependencies from the appropriate injectors in it.

Using the @Self decorator

Now let's suppose we have the following configuration:

```
abstract class Channel {}
class Http extends Channel {}
class WebSocket extends Channel {}

@Injectable()
class UserService {
  constructor(public channel: Channel) {}
```

```
}

let parentInjector = ReflectiveInjector.resolveAndCreate([
  { provide: Channel, useClass: Http }
]);
let childInjector = parentInjector.resolveAndCreateChild([
  {  provide: Channel, useClass: WebSocket },
  UserService
]);
```

We can instantiate the UserService token using:

```
childInjector.get(UserService);
```

In UserService, we can declare that we want to get the Channel dependency from the current injector (that is, childInjector) using the @Self decorator:

```
@Injectable()
class UserService {
  constructor(@Self() public channel: Channel) {}
}
```

Although this is going to be the default behavior during the instantiation of the UserService, using @Self, we can be more explicit. Let's suppose we change the configuration of childInjector to the following:

```
let parentInjector = ReflectiveInjector.resolveAndCreate([
  { provide: Channel, useClass: Http }
]);
let childInjector = parentInjector.resolveAndCreateChild([
  UserService
]);
```

If we keep the @Self decorator in the UserService constructor and try to instantiate UserService using childInjector, we will get a runtime error because of the missing provider for Channel.

Skipping the self injector

In some cases, especially while injecting the dependencies of UI components, we may want to use the provider registered in the parent injector instead of the one registered in the current injector. We can achieve this behavior by taking advantage of the @SkipSelf decorator. For instance, let's suppose we have the following definition of the class Context:

```
class Context {
  constructor(public parentContext: Context) {}
}
```

Each instance of the `Context` class has a parent. Now let's build a hierarchy of two injectors, which will allow us to create a context with a parent context:

```
let parentInjector = ReflectiveInjector.resolveAndCreate([
  { provide: Context, useValue: new Context(null) }
]);
let childInjector = parentInjector.resolveAndCreateChild([
  Context
]);
```

Since the root context doesn't have a parent, we will set the value of its provider to be `new Context(null)`.

If we want to instantiate the child context, we can use:

```
childInjector.get(Context);
```

For the instantiation of the child, `Context` will be used by the provider registered within the `childInjector`. However, as a dependency it accepts an object which is an instance of the `Context` class. Such classes exist in the same injector, which means that Angular will try to instantiate it, but it has a dependency of the `Context` type. This process will lead to an infinite loop that will cause a runtime error.

In order to prevent it from happening, we can change the definition of `Context` in the following way:

```
class Context {
  constructor(@SkipSelf() public parentContext: Context) {}
}
```

The only change that we introduced is the addition of the parameter decorator `@SkipSelf`.

Having optional dependencies

Angular 2 introduces the `@Optional` decorator, which allows us to deal with dependencies that don't have a registered provider associated with them. Suppose a dependency of a provider is not available in any of the target injectors responsible for its instantiation. If we use the `@Optional` decorator, during the instantiation of the dependent provider for value of the missing dependency will be passed `null`.

Now let's take a look at the following example:

```
abstract class SortingAlgorithm {
  abstract sort(collection: BaseCollection): BaseCollection;
}
```

```
@Injectable()
class Collection extends BaseCollection {
  private sort: SortingAlgorithm;
  constructor(sort: SortingAlgorithm) {
    super();
    this.sort = sort || this.getDefaultSort();
  }
}

let injector = ReflectiveInjector.resolveAndCreate([
  Collection
]);
```

In this case, we defined an abstract class called SortingAlgorithm and a class called Collection, which accepts an instance of a concrete class as a dependency that extends SortingAlgorithm. Inside of the Collection constructor, we set the sort instance property to the passed dependency of the SortingAlgorithm type or a default sorting algorithm implementation.

We didn't define any providers for the SortingAlgorithm token in the injector we configured. So, if we want to get an instance of the Collection class using injector.get(Collection), we'll get a runtime error. This means that if we want to get an instance of the Collection class using the DI mechanism of the framework, we must register a provider for the SortingAlgorithm token, although we can fall back to the default sorting algorithm's implementation.

Angular 2 provides a solution to this problem with the @Optional decorator.

This is how we can approach the problem using the @Optional decorator provided by the framework:

```
// ch5/ts/decorators/optional.ts
@Injectable()
class Collection extends BaseCollection {
  private sort: SortingAlgorithm;
  constructor(@Optional() sort: SortingAlgorithm) {
    super();
    this.sort = sort || this.getDefaultSort();
  }
}
```

In the preceding snippet, we declared the sort dependency as optional, which means that if Angular 2 doesn't find any provider for its token, it will pass the null value.

Using multiproviders

Multiproviders are another new concept brought to the Angular 2 DI mechanism. They allow us to associate multiple providers with the same token. This can be quite useful if we're developing a third-party library that comes with some default implementations of different services, but you want to allow the users to extend it with custom ones. They are also exclusively used to declare multiple validations over a single control in the Angular 2 form module. We will explain this module in Chapter 6, *Angular 2 forms and the new component-based router*, and Chapter 7, *Building a real-life application while exploring pipes and http*.

Another sample of an applicable use case of multiproviders is what Angular 2 uses for event management in their WebWorkers implementation. They create multiproviders for event management plugins. Each of the providers returns a different strategy, which supports a different set of events (touch events, keyboard events, and so on). Once a given event occurs, they can choose the appropriate plugin that handles it.

Let's take a look at an example that illustrates the typical usage of multiproviders:

```
// ch5/ts/configuring-providers/multi-providers.ts
const VALIDATOR = new OpaqueToken('validator');

interface EmployeeValidator {
  (person: Employee): boolean;
}

class Employee {...}

let injector = ReflectiveInjector.resolveAndCreate([
  { provide: VALIDATOR, multi: true,
    useValue: (person: Employee) => {
      if (!person.name) {
        return 'The name is required';
      }
    }
  },
  { provide: VALIDATOR, multi: true,
    useValue: (person: Employee) => {
      if (!person.name || person.name.length < 1) {
        return 'The name should be more than 1 symbol long';
      }
    }
  },
  Employee
]);
```

In the preceding snippet, we declared a constant called VALIDATOR with a new instance of OpaqueToken. We also created an injector where we registered three providers—two of them are used as value functions that, based on different criteria, validate instances of the class Employee. These functions are of the type EmployeeValidator.

In order to declare that we want the injector to pass all the registered validators to the constructor of the class Employee, we need to use the following constructor definition:

```
class Employee {
  name: string;
  constructor(@Inject(VALIDATOR) private validators:
EmployeeValidator[]) {}
  validate() {
    return this.validators
      .map(v => v(this))
      .filter(value => !!value);
  }
}
```

In the preceding example, we declared a class Employee that accepts a single dependency—an array of EmployeeValidators. In the method validate, we applied the individual validators over the current class instance and filtered the results in order to get only the ones that have returned an error message.

Notice that the constructor argument validators is of the EmployeeValidator[] type. Since we can't use the type "array of objects" as a token for a provider, because it is not a valid type reference, we need to use the @Inject parameter decorator.

Using DI with components and directives

In Chapter 4, *Getting Started with Angular 2 Components and Directives*, when we developed our first Angular 2 directive, we saw how we can take advantage of the DI mechanism to inject services into our UI-related components (that is, directives and components).

Let's take a quick look at what we did earlier, but from a DI perspective:

```
// ch4/ts/tooltip/app.ts
// ...
@Directive(...)
export class Tooltip {
  @Input()
  saTooltip:string;

  constructor(private el: ElementRef, private overlay: Overlay) {
```

```
        this.overlay.attach(el.nativeElement);
    }
    // ...
}
@Component({
    // ...
    providers: [Overlay],
    directives: [Tooltip]
})
class App {}
```

Most of the code from the earlier implementation is omitted because it is not directly related to our current focus.

Note that the constructor of `Tooltip` accepts two dependencies:

- An instance of the `ElementRef` class.
- An instance of the `Overlay` class.

The types of dependencies are the tokens associated with their providers, and the corresponding values from the providers are going to be injected with the DI mechanism of Angular 2.

Although the declaration of the dependencies of the `Tooltip` class looks exactly the same as what we did in the previous sections, there's neither any explicit configuration nor any instantiation of an injector.

Introducing the element injectors

Under the hood, Angular will create injectors for all the directives and components, and add a default set of providers to it. This is the so-called **element injector** and is something the framework takes care of itself. The injectors associated with the components are called **host injectors**. One of the providers in each directive and component injector is associated with the `ElementRef` token; it will return a reference to the host element of the directive. But where is the provider for the `Overlay` class declared? Let's take a look at the implementation of the top-level component:

```
@Component({
    // ...
    providers: [Overlay],
    directives: [Tooltip]
})

class App {}
```

We configured the element injector for the App component by declaring the providers property inside of the @Component decorator. At this point, the registered providers are going to be visible by the directive or the component associated with the corresponding element injector and the component's entire component subtree, unless it is overridden somewhere in the hierarchy.

Declaring providers for the element injectors

Having the declaration of all the providers in the same place might be quite inconvenient. For example, imagine we're developing a large-scale application that has hundreds of components depending on thousands of services. In this case, configuring all the providers in the root component is not a practical solution. There will be name collisions when two or more providers are associated to the same token. The configuration will be huge and it will be hard to trace where the different tokens need to be injected.

As we mentioned, Angular 2's @Directive (and respectively @Component) decorator allows us to introduce directive-specific providers using the providers property. Here is how we can approach this:

```
@Directive({
  selector: '[saTooltip]',
  providers: [OverlayMock]
})
export class Tooltip {
 @Input() saTooltip: string;

  constructor(private el: ElementRef, private overlay: Overlay) {
    this.overlay.attach(el.nativeElement);
  }
  // ...
}

// ...

bootstrap(App);
```

The preceding example overrides the provider for the Overlay token in the Tooltip directive's declaration. This way, Angular will inject an instance of OverlayMock instead of Overlay during the instantiation of the tooltip.

A better way to override the provider is using the `bootstrap` function. We can do the following:

```
bootstrap(AppMock, [{ provide: Overlay,
  useClass: OverlayMock
}]);
```

In the preceding `bootstrap` call, we provided a different top-level component and provider for the `Overlay` service that will return an instance of the `OverlayMock` class. This way, we can test the `Tooltip` directive ignoring the implementation of `Overlay`.

Exploring DI with components

Since components are generally directives with views, everything we've seen so far regarding how the DI mechanism works with directives is valid for components as well. However, because of the extra features that the components provide, we're allowed to have further control over their providers.

As we said, the injector associated with each component will be marked as a **host** injector. There's a parameter decorator called `@Host`, which allows us to retrieve a given dependency from any injector until it reaches the closest host injector. This means that by using the `@Host` decorator in a directive, we can declare that we want to retrieve the given dependency from the current injector or any parent injector until we reach the injector of the closest parent component.

The `viewProviders` property added to the `@Component` decorator is in charge of achieving even more control.

viewProviders versus providers

Let's take a look at an example of a component called `MarkdownPanel`. This component will be used in the following way:

```
<markdown-panel>
  <panel-title># Title</pane-title>
  <panel-content>
# Content of the panel
* First point
* Second point

  </panel-content>

</markdown-panel>
```

The content of each section of the panel will be translated from the markdown to the HTML. We can delegate this functionality to a service called `Markdown`:

```
import * as markdown from 'markdown';
class Markdown {
  toHTML(md) {
    return markdown.toHTML(md);
  }
}
```

The `Markdown` service wraps the markdown module in order to make it injectable through the DI mechanism.

Now let's implement `MarkdownPanel`.

In the following snippet, we can find all the important details from the component's implementation:

```
// ch5/ts/directives/app.ts
@Component({
  selector: 'markdown-panel',
  viewProviders: [Markdown],
  styles: [...],
  template: `
    <div class="panel">
      <div class="panel-title">
        <ng-content select="panel-title"></ng-content>
      </div>
      <div class="panel-content">
        <ng-content select="panel-content"></ng-content>
      </div>
    </div>`
})
class MarkdownPanel {
  constructor(private el: ElementRef, private md: Markdown) {}
  ngAfterContentInit() {
    let el = this.el.nativeElement;
    let title = el.querySelector('panel-title');
    let content = el.querySelector('panel-content');
    title.innerHTML = this.md.toHTML(title.innerHTML);
    content.innerHTML = this.md.toHTML(content.innerHTML);
  }
}
```

We used the `markdown-panel` selector and set the `viewProviders` property. In this case, there's only a single view provider: the one for the `Markdown` service. By setting this property, we declared that all the providers declared in it will be accessible from the component itself and all of its **view children**.

Now, let's suppose we have a component called `MarkdownButton` and we want to add it to our template in the following way:

```
<markdown-panel>
  <panel-title>### Small title</panel-title>
  <panel-content>
  Some code
  </panel-content>
  <markdown-button>*Click to toggle*</markdown-button>
</markdown-panel>
```

The `Markdown` service will not be accessible by the `MarkdownButton` used below the `panel-content` element; however, it'll be accessible if we use the button in the component's template:

```
@Component({
  selector: 'markdown-panel',
  viewProviders: [Markdown],
  directives: [MarkdownButton],
  styles: [...],
  template: `
    <div class="panel">
      <markdown-button>*Click to toggle*</markdown-button>
      <div class="panel-title">
        <ng-content select="panel-title"></ng-content>
      </div>
      <div class="panel-content">
        <ng-content select="panel-content"></ng-content>
      </div>
    </div>`
})
```

If we need the provider to be visible in all the content and view children, all we should do is change the property name of the `viewProviders` property to `providers`.

You can find this example in the file in the examples directory at `ch5/ts/directives/app.ts`.

Using Angular's DI with ES5

We are already proficient in using the dependency injection of Angular 2 with TypeScript! As we know, we are not limited to TypeScript for the development of Angular 2 applications; we can also use ES5, ES2015, and ES2016 (as well as Dart, but that is out of the scope of this book).

So far, we declared the dependencies of the different classes in their constructor using standard TypeScript type annotations. All such classes are supposed to be decorated with the @Injectable decorator. Unfortunately, some of the other languages supported by Angular 2 miss a few of these features. In the following table, we can see that ES5 doesn't support type annotations, classes, and decorators:

	ES5	ES2015	ES2016
Classes	No	Yes	Yes
Decorators	No	No	Yes (no parameter decorators)
Type annotations	No	No	No

In this case, how we can take advantage of the DI mechanism in these languages? Angular 2 provides an internal JavaScript **Domain Specific Language (DSL)**, which allows us to take advantage of the entire functionality of the framework using ES5.

Now, let's translate the MarkdownPanel example we took a look at in the previous section from TypeScript to ES5. First, let's start with the Markdown service:

```
// ch5/es5/simple-example/app.js
var Markdown = ng.core.Class({
  constructor: function () {},
  toHTML: function (md) {
    return markdown.toHTML(md);
  }
});
```

We defined a variable called Markdown and set its value to the returned result from the invocation of ng.core.Class. This construct allows us to emulate ES2015 classes using ES5. The argument of the ng.core.Class method is an object literal, which must have the definition of a constructor function. As a result, ng.core.Class will return a JavaScript constructor function with the body of constructor from the object literal. All the other methods defined within the boundaries of the passed parameter will be added to the function's prototype.

One problem is solved: we can now emulate classes in ES5; there are two more problems left!

Now, let's take a look at how we can define the `MarkdownPanel` component:

```
// ch5/es5/simple-example/app.js

var MarkdownPanel = ng.core.Component({
  selector: 'markdown-panel',
  viewProviders: [Markdown],
  styles: [...],
  template: '...'
})
.Class({
  constructor: [Markdown, ng.core.ElementRef, function (md, el) {
    this.md = md;
    this.el = el;
  }],
  ngAfterContentInit: function () {
    ...
  }
});
```

From *Chapter 4, Getting Started with Angular 2 Components and Directives*, we are already familiar with the ES5 syntax used to define components. Now, let's take a look at the constructor function of `MarkdownPanel` in order to make sure how we can declare the dependencies of our components and even classes in general.

From the preceding snippet, we can note that the value of the constructor is not a function this time, but an array instead. This might seem familiar to you from AngularJS 1.x, where we are able to declare the dependencies of the given service by listing their names:

```
Module.service('UserMapper',
  ['User', '$http', function (User, $http) {
    // …
  }]);
```

Although the syntax in Angular 2 is similar, it brings a lot of improvements. For instance, we're no longer limited to using strings for the dependencies' tokens.

Now, let's suppose we want to make the `Markdown` service an optional dependency. In this case, we can approach this by passing an array of decorators:

```
...
.Class({
  constructor: [[ng.core.Optional(), Markdown],
    ng.core.ElementRef, function (md, el) {
```

```
        this.md = md;
        this.el = el;
    }],
  ngAfterContentInit: function () {
    …
  }
});
…
```

This way, by nesting arrays, we can apply a sequence of decorators: `[[ng.core.Optional(),ng.core.Self(),Markdown],...]`. In this example, the `@Optional` and `@Self` decorators will add the associated metadata to the class in the specified order.

Although using ES5 makes our build simpler and allows us to skip the intermediate step of transpilation, which can be tempting, Google's recommendation is to take advantage of static typing using TypeScript. This way, we have a much clearer syntax, which carries better semantics with less typing and provides us with great tooling.

Summary

In this chapter, we covered the DI mechanism of Angular 2. We briefly discussed the positives of using dependency injection in our projects by introducing it in the context of the framework. The second step in our journey was how to instantiate and configure injectors; we also explained the injectors' hierarchy and the visibility of the registered providers. In order to enforce a better separation of concerns, we mentioned how we can inject services carrying the business logic of our application in our directives and components. The last point we took a look at was how we can use the DI mechanism with the ES5 syntax.

In the next chapter, we'll introduce the new routing mechanism of the framework. We'll explain how we can configure the component-based router and add multiple views to our application. Another important topic we are going to cover is the new form module. By building a simple application, we will demonstrate how we can create and manage forms.

6
Working with the Angular 2 Router and Forms

By now, we're already familiar with the core of the framework. We know how to define components and directives in order to develop the view of our applications. We also know how to encapsulate business-related logic into services and wire everything together with the dependency injection mechanism of Angular 2.

 Note that the forms and router modules explained in the following section are now deprecated. Although they will be replaced with different implementations which have different APIs, they share the same foundational idea and follow similar approach. I strongly recommend you to explore this chapter in order to get better under-standing of how these modules work.

In this chapter, we'll explain a few more concepts that will help us build real-life Angular 2 applications. They are as follows:

- The component-based router of the framework.
- Using Angular 2 forms.
- Developing template-driven forms.
- Developing custom form validators.

Let's begin!

Developing the "Coders repository" application

In the process of explaining the concepts mentioned earlier, we'll develop a sample application that contains a repository of developers. Before we start coding, let's explain the structure of the application.

The "Coders repository" will allow its users to add developers either by filling a form with details about them or by providing the GitHub handle for the developer and importing his or her profile from GitHub.

 For the purpose of this chapter, we will store information on the developers in memory, which means that after the page is refreshed, we'll lose all the stored during the session data.

The application will have the following views:

- A list of all the developers.
- A view that adds or imports new developers.
- A view that shows the given developer's details. This view has two subviews:
  - **Basic details**: Shows the name of the developer and her or his GitHub avatar if available.
  - **Advanced profile**: Shows all the details known for the developer.

The end result of the home page of the application will look as follows:

GitHub handle	Email	Real name	Technology	Popular
mhevery	misko@hevery.com	Miško Hevery		Yes
addyosmani	addyosmani@gmail.com	Addy Osmani		Yes
	josh@example.com	Josh Long	C#	No

Browser window showing: *Switching to Angular 2* — localhost:5555/dist/dev/ch7/ts/multi-page-model-driven/ — Home   Add developer

Fig. 1

In this chapter, we will build only a few of the listed views. The rest of the application will be explained in *Chapter 7, Explaining Pipes and Communicating with RESTful Services.*

Each developer will be an instance of the following class:

```
// ch6/ts/multi-page-template-driven/developer.ts
export class Developer {
  public id: number;
  public githubHandle: string;
  public avatarUrl: string;
  public realName: string;
  public email: string;
  public technology: string;
  public popular: boolean;
}
```

All the developers will reside within the DeveloperCollection class:

```
// ch6/ts/multi-page-template-driven/developer_collection.ts
class DeveloperCollection {
  private developers: Developer[] = [];
  getUserByGitHubHandle(username: string) {
    return this.developers
            .filter(u => u.githubHandle === username)
            .pop();
  }
  getUserById(id: number) {
    return this.developers
            .filter(u => u.id === id)
            .pop();
  }
  addDeveloper(dev: Developer) {
    this.developers.push(dev);
  }
  getAll() {
    return this.developers;
  }
}
```

The classes mentioned here encapsulate quite a simple logic and don't have anything Angular 2-specific, so we won't get into any details.

Now, let's continue with the implementation by exploring the new router.

Exploring the Angular 2 router

As we already know, in order to bootstrap any Angular 2 application, we need to develop a root component. The "Coders repository" application is not any different; the only addition in this specific case is that we will have multiple pages that need to be connected together with the Angular 2 router.

Let's start with the imports required for the router's configuration and define the root component right after this:

```
// ch6/ts/step-0/app.ts
import {
 HashLocationStrategy,
 LocationStrategy
} '@angular/common';
import {
  ROUTER_DIRECTIVES,
  ROUTER_PROVIDERS,
  Route,
  Redirect,
  RouteConfig
} from '@angular/router-deprecated';
```

In the preceding snippet, we imported a couple of things directly from the Angular 2 router module, which is externalized outside the framework's core.

With ROUTER_DIRECTIVES, the router provides a set of commonly used directives that we can add to the list of used ones by the root component. This way, we will be able to use them in the templates later.

The import ROUTE_PROVIDERS contains a set of router-related providers, such as one for injecting the RouteParams token into the components' constructors.

The RouteParams token provides an access to parameters from the route's URL in order to parametrize the logic associated with a given page. We'll demonstrate a typical use case of this provider later.

The import LocationStrategy class is an abstract class that defines the common logic between HashLocationStrategy (used for hash-based routing) and PathLocationStrategy (used for HTML5-based routing by taking advantage of the history API).

HashLocationStrategy does not support server-side rendering. This is due to the fact that the hash of the page does not get sent to the server, so it cannot find out the component associated with the given page. All modern browsers except IE9 support the HTML5 history API. You can find more about server-side rendering in the last chapter of the book.

The last imports we didn't take a look at are RouteConfig, which is a decorator that allows us to define the routes associated with a given component; and Route and Redirect, which respectively allow us to define the individual routes and redirects. With RouteConfig, we can define a hierarchy of routes, which means that the router of Angular 2 supports nested routing out of the box unlike its predecessor in AngularJS 1.x.

Defining the root component and bootstrapping the application

Now, let's define a root component and configure the application's initial bootstrap:

```
// ch6/ts/step-0/app.ts
@Component({
  selector: 'app',
  template: `...`,
  providers: [DeveloperCollection],
  directives: [ROUTER_DIRECTIVES]
})
@RouteConfig([...])
class App {}

bootstrap(...);
```

In the preceding snippet, you can notice a syntax we're already familiar with from *Chapter 4, Getting Started with Angular 2 Components and Directives* and *Chapter 5, Dependency Injection in Angular 2*. We defined a component with an app selector, template that we're going to take a look at later, and sets of providers and directives.

The App component uses a single provider called DeveloperCollection. This is the class that contains all the developers stored by the application. You can notice that we added ROUTER_DIRECTIVES; it contains an array of all the directives defined within the Angular's router. Some of the directives within this array allow us to link to the other routes defined within the @RouteConfig decorator (the routerLink directive) and declare the place where the components associated with the different routes should be rendered (router-outlet). We'll explain how we can use them later in this section.

Now let's take a look at the call of the `bootstrap` function:

```
bootstrap(App, [
  ROUTER_PROVIDERS,
  { provide: LocationStrategy, useClass: HashLocationStrategy }
)]);
```

As the first argument of `bootstrap`, we pass the root component of the application as usual. The second argument is a list of providers that will be accessible by the entire application. To the set of providers, we add ROUTER_PROVIDERS and we also configure the provider for the `LocationStrategy` token. The default `LocationStrategy` token, which Angular 2 uses, is `PathLocationStrategy` (that is, the HTML5-based one). However, in this case, we are going to use the hash-based one.

The two biggest advantages of the default location strategy are that it is supported by the server-rendering module of Angular 2, and the application's URL looks more natural to the end user (there's no # used). On the other hand, in case we use `PathLocationStrategy`, we may need to configure our application server, in order to handle the routes properly.

Using PathLocationStrategy

If we want to use `PathLocationStrategy`, we may need to provide APP_BASE_HREF. For instance, in our case, the `bootstrap` configuration should look as follows:

```
import {APP_BASE_HREF} from '@angular/common';
//...
bootstrap(App, [
  ROUTER_PROVIDERS,
  // The following line is optional, since it's
  // the default value for the LocationStrategy token
  { provide: LocationStrategy, useClass: PathLocationStrategy },
  { provide: APP_BASE_HREF,
    useValue: '/dist/dev/ch6/ts/multi-page-template-driven/'
  }
]);
```

By default, the value associated with the APP_BASE_HREF token is /; it represents the base path name inside of the application. For instance, in our case, the "Coders repository" will be located under the /ch6/ts/multi-page-template-driven/ directory (that is, http://localhost:5555/dist/dev/ch6/ts/multi-page-template-driven/).

Configuring routes with @RouteConfig

As the next step, let's take a look at the route's declaration placed in the @RouteConfig decorator:

```
// ch6/ts/step-0/app.ts
@Component(...)
@RouteConfig([
  new Route({ component: Home, name: 'Home', path: '/' }),
  new Route({
    component: AddDeveloper,
    name: 'AddDeveloper',
    path: '/dev-add'
  }),
  //...
  new Redirect({
    path: '/add-dev',
    redirectTo: ['/dev-add']
  })
])
class App {}
```

As the preceding snippet shows, the @RouteConfig decorator accepts an array of routes as an argument. In the example, we defined two types of routes: using the classes Route and Redirect. They are used respectively to define the routes and redirects in the application.

Each route must define the following properties:

- component: The component associated with the given route.
- name: The name of the route used for referencing it in the templates.
- path: The path to be used for the route. It will be visible in the browser's location bar.

 The Route class also supports a data property whose value can be injected in the constructor of its associated component by using the RouteData token. A sample use case of the data property could be if we want to inject different configuration objects based on the type of the parent component that contains the @RouteConfig declaration.

On the other hand, the redirect contains only two properties:

- `path`: The path to be used for the redirection.
- `redirectTo`: The path the user is redirected to.

In the previous example, we declared that we want the page opened by the user with the path `/add-dev` to be redirected to `['/dev-add']`.

Now, in order to make everything work, we need to define the `AddDeveloper` and `Home` components, which are referenced in `@RouteConfig`. Initially, we're going to provide a basic implementation that we'll incrementally extend over time along the chapter. In `ch6/ts/step-0`, create a file called `home.ts` and enter the following content:

```
import {Component} from '@angular/core';
@Component({
  selector: 'home',
  template: `Home`
})
export class Home {}
```

Do not forget to import the `Home` component in `app.ts`. Now, open the file called `add_developer.ts` and enter the following content in it:

```
import {Component} from '@angular/core';

@Component({
  selector: 'dev-add',
  template: `Add developer`
})
export class AddDeveloper {}
```

Using routerLink and router-outlet

We have the route's declaration and all the components associated with the individual routes. The only thing left is to define the template of the root `App` component in order to link everything together.

Add the following content to the `template` property inside the `@Component` decorator in `ch6/ts/step-0/app.ts`:

```
@Component({
  //...
  template: `
    <nav class="navbar navbar-default">
      <ul class="nav navbar-nav">
        <li><a [routerLink]="['/Home']">Home</a></li>
        <li><a [routerLink]="['/AddDeveloper']">Add developer</a></li>
      </ul>
    </nav>
    <router-outlet></router-outlet>
  `,
  //...
})
```

In the template above there are two Angular 2-specific directives:

- `routerLink`: This allows us to add a link to a specific route.
- `router-outlet`: This defines the container where the components associated with the currently selected route need to be rendered.

Let's take a look at the `routerLink` directive. As value it accepts an array of route names and parameters. In our case we provide only a single route name prefixed with slash (since this route is on root level). Notice that the route name used by `routerLink` is declared by the `name` property of the route declaration inside `@RouteConfig`. Later in this chapter we'll see how we can link to nested routes and pass route parameters.

This directive allows us to declare links independently from `LocationStrategy` that we have configured. For instance, imagine we are using `HashLocationStrategy`; this means that we need to prefix all the routes in our templates with #. In case we switch to `PathLocationStrategy`, we'll need to remove all the hash prefixes. Another huge benefit of `routerLink` is that it uses the HTML5 history push API transparently to us, which saves us from a lot of boilerplates.

The next directive from the previous template that is new to us is `router-outlet`. It has similar responsibility to the `ng-view` directive in AngularJS 1.x. Basically, they both have the same role: to point out where the `target` component should be rendered. This means that according to the definition, when the user navigates to /, the `Home` component will be rendered at the position pointed out by `router-outlet`, same for the `AddDeveloper` component once the user navigates to `/dev-add`.

Now we have these two routes up and running! Open `http://localhost:5555/dist/dev/ch6/ts/step-0/` and you should see the following screenshot:

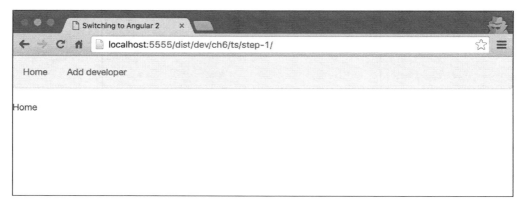

Fig. 2

If you don't, just take a look at `ch6/ts/step-1` that contains the end result.

Lazy-loading with AsyncRoute

AngularJS 1.x modules allow us to group together logically related units in the application. However, by default, they need to be available during the initial application's `bootstrap` and do not allow deferred loading. This requires downloading the entire codebase of the application during the initial page load that, in case of large single-page apps, can be an unacceptable performance hit.

In a perfect scenario, we would want to load only the code associated with the page the user is currently viewing, or to prefetch bundled modules based on heuristics related to the user's behavior, which is out of the scope of this book. For instance, open the application from the first step of our example: `http://localhost:5555/dist/dev/ch6/ts/step-1/`. Once the user is at `/`, we only need the `Home` component to be available, and once he or she navigates to `/dev-add`, we want to load the `AddDeveloper` component.

Let's inspect what is actually going on in Chrome DevTools:

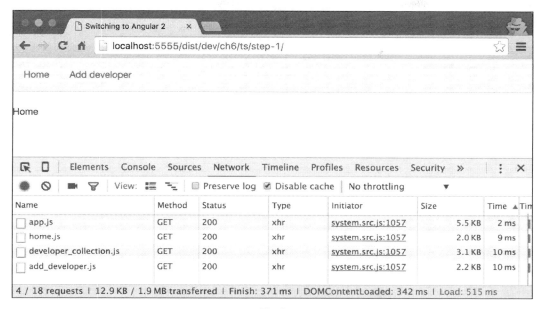

Fig. 3

We can notice that during the initial page load, we downloaded the components associated with all the routes, even AddDeveloper that is not required. This happens because in app.ts, we explicitly require both the Home and the AddDeveloper components and use them in the @RouteConfig declaration.

In this specific case, loading both the components may not seem like a big problem, because at this step, they are pretty simple and do not have any dependencies. However, in real-life applications, they will have imports of other directives, components, pipes, services, or even third-party libraries. Once any of the components is required, its entire dependency graph will be downloaded, even if the component is not needed at that point.

The router of Angular 2 comes with a solution to this problem. All we need to do is import the AsyncRoute class from the @angular/router-deprecated module and use it inside @RouteConfig instead of using Route:

```
// ch6/ts/step-1-async/app.ts

import {AsyncRoute} from '@angular/router-deprecated';
@Component (...)
@RouteConfig ([
  new AsyncRoute ({
    loader: () =>
      System.import ('./home')
        .then (m => m.Home),
    name: 'Home',
    path: '/'
  }),
  new AsyncRoute ({
    loader: () =>
      System.import ('./add_developer')
        .then (m => m.AddDeveloper),
    name: 'AddDeveloper',
    path: '/dev-add'
  }),
    new Redirect ({ path: '/add-dev', redirectTo: ['/dev-add'] })
])
class App {}
```

The constructor of the AsyncRoute class accepts as an argument an object with the following properties:

- loader: A function that returns a promise that needs to be resolved with the component associated with the given route.

- name: The name of the route that can be used to refer to it in the templates (usually, inside of the routerLink directive).

- path: The path of the route.

Once the user navigates to a route that matches any of the async routes' definitions in the `@RouteConfig` decorator, its associated loader will be invoked. When the promise returned by the loader is resolved with a value of the target component, the component will be cached and rendered. Next time the user navigates to the same route, the cached component will be used, so the routing module won't download the same component twice.

 Notice that the preceding example uses System, however, Angular's `AsyncRoute` implementation is not coupled to any particular module loader. The same result could be achieved, for instance, with require.js.

Using Angular 2 forms

Now let's continue with the implementation of the application. For the next step, we'll work on the `AddDeveloper` and `Home` components. You can continue your implementation by extending what you currently have in `ch6/ts/step-0`, or if you haven't reached step 1 yet, you can keep working on the files in `ch6/ts/step-1`.

Angular 2 offers two ways to develop forms with validation:

- **A template-driven approach**: Provides a declarative API where we declare the validations into the template of the component.
- **A model-driven approach**: Provides an imperative API with `FormBuilder`.

In the next chapter, we'll explore both. Let's start with the template-driven approach.

Developing template-driven forms

Forms are essential for each **CRUD (Create Retrieve Update and Delete)** application. In our case, we want to build a form for entering the details of the developers we want to store.

By the end of this section, we'll have a form that allows us to enter the real name of a given developer, to add his or her preferred technology, enter an e-mail, and declare whether she or he is popular in the community or not yet. The end result will look as follows:

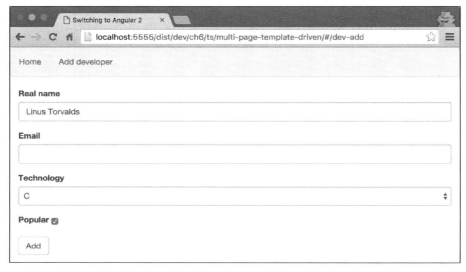

Fig. 4

Add the following imports to add_developer.ts:

```
import {
  FORM_DIRECTIVES,
  FORM_PROVIDERS
} from '@angular/common;
```

The next thing we need to do is add FORM_DIRECTIVES to the list of directives used by the AddDeveloper component. The FORM_DIRECTIVES directives contains a set of predefined directives for managing Angular 2 forms, such as the form and ngModel directives.

The FORM_PROVIDERS is an array with a predefined set of providers that we can use for injecting the values associated with their tokens in the classes of our application.

Now update the AddDeveloper implementation to the following:

```
@Component({
  selector: 'dev-add',
  templateUrl: './add_developer.html',
  styles: […],
```

```
    directives: [FORM_DIRECTIVES],
    providers: [FORM_PROVIDERS]
})
export class AddDeveloper {
  developer = new Developer();
  errorMessage: string;
  successMessage: string;
  submitted = false;
  technologies: string[] = [
    'JavaScript',
    'C',
    'C#',
    'Clojure'
  ];
  constructor(private developers: DeveloperCollection) {}
  addDeveloper() {}
}
```

The `developer` property contains the information associated with the current developer that we're adding with the form. The last two properties, `errorMessage` and `successMessage`, are going to be used respectively for displaying the current form's error or success messages once the developer has been successfully added to the developers collection, or an error has occurred.

Digging into the template-driven form's markup

As the next step, let's create the template of the `AddDeveloper` component (`step-1/add_developer.html`). Add the following content to the file:

```
<span *ngIf="errorMessage"
      class="alert alert-danger">{{errorMessage}}</span>
<span *ngIf="successMessage"
      class="alert alert-success">{{successMessage}}</span>
```

These two elements are intended to display the error and success messages when adding a new developer. They are going to be visible when `errorMessage` and `successMessage` respectively have non-falsy values (that is, something different from the empty string, `false`, `undefined`, `0`, `NaN`, or `null`).

Now let's develop the actual form:

```
<form #f="ngForm" (ngSubmit)="addDeveloper()"
      class="form col-md-4" [hidden]="submitted">
  <div class="form-group">
    <label class="control-label"
           for="realNameInput">Real name</label>
    <div>
      <input id="realNameInput" class="form-control"
             type="text" ngControl="realName" required
             [(ngModel)]="developer.realName">
    </div>
  </div>
  <button class="btn btn-default"
          type="submit" [disabled]="!f.form.valid">Add</button>
  <!-- MORE CODE TO BE ADDED -->
</form>
```

We declare a new form using the HTML `form` tag. Once Angular 2 finds such tags in a template with an included form directive in the parent component, it will automatically enhance its functionality in order to be used as an Angular form. Once the form is processed by Angular, we can apply form validation and data-bindings. After this, using `#f="ngForm"`, we will define a local variable for the template called `f`, which allows us to reference to the current form. The last thing left from the form element is the submit event handler. We use a syntax that we're already familiar with `(ngSubmit)="expr"`, where in this case, the value of the expression is the call of the `addDeveloper` method attached to the component's controller.

Now, let's take a look at the `div` element with class name `control-group`.

 Note that this is not an Angular-specific class; it is a CSS class defined by Bootstrap that we use in order to provide a better look and feel to the form.

Inside of it, we can find a `label` element that doesn't have any Angular-specific markup and an input element that allows us to set the real name of the current developer. We set the control to be of a type text and declare its identifier to equal `realNameInput`. The required attribute is defined by the HTML5 specification and is used for validation. By using it on the element, we declare that it is required for this element to have a value. Although this attribute is not Angular-specific using the `ngControl` attribute, Angular will extend the semantics of the required attribute by including validation behavior. This behavior includes setting specific CSS classes on the control when its status changes and managing its state that the framework keeps internally.

The `ngControl` directive is a selector of the `NgControlName` directive. It enhances the behavior of the form controls by running validation over them for the change of their values, and applying specific classes during the controls' life cycle. You might be familiar with this from AngularJS 1.x where the form controls are decorated with the `ng-pristine`, `ng-invalid`, and `ng-valid` classes, and so on, in specific phases of their lifecycle.

The following table summarizes the CSS classes that the framework adds to the form controls during their lifecycle:

Classes	Description
ng-untouched	The control hasn't been visited
ng-touched	The control has been visited
ng-pristine	The control's value hasn't been changed
ng-dirty	The control's value has been changed
ng-valid	All the validators attached to the control have returned `true`
ng-invalid	Any of the validators attached to the control has a `false` value

According to this table, we can define that we want all the input controls with invalid value to have a red border in the following way:

```
input.ng-dirty.ng-invalid {
  border: 1px solid red;
}
```

The exact semantics behind the preceding CSS in the context of Angular 2 is to use a red border for all the input elements whose values have been changed and are invalid according to the validators attached to them.

Now, let's explore how we can attach different validation behavior to our controls.

Using the built-in form validators

We already saw that we can alter validation behavior to any control by using the `required` attribute. Angular 2 provides two more built-in validators, as follows:

- `minlength`: Allows us to specify the minimum length of the value that a given control should have.

- `maxlength`: Allows us to specify the maximum length of the value that a given control should have.

These validators are defined with Angular 2 directives and can be used in the following way:

```
<input id="realNameInput" class="form-control"
       type="text" ngControl="realName"
       minlength="2"
       maxlength="30">
```

This way, we specify that we want the value of the input to be between 2 and 30 characters.

Defining custom control validators

Another data property defined in the `Developer` class is the `email` field. Let's add an input field for this property. Above the button in the preceding form, add the following markup:

```
<div class="form-group">
  <label class="control-label" for="emailInput">Email</label>
  <div>
    <input id="emailInput"
           class="form-control"
           type="text" ngControl="email"
      [(ngModel)]="developer.email">
  </div>
</div>
```

We can think of the `[(ngModel)]` attribute as an alternative to the `ng-model` directive from AngularJS 1.x. We will explain it in detail in the *Two-way data binding with Angular 2* section.

Although Angular 2 provides a set of predefined validators, they are not enough for all the various formats our data can live in. Sometimes, we'll need custom validation logic for our application-specific data. For instance, in this case, we want to define an e-mail validator. A typical regular expression, which works in general cases (but does not cover the entire specification that defines the format of the e-mail addresses), looks as follows: `/^[a-zA-Z0-9_.+-]+@[a-zA-Z0-9-]+\.[a-zA-Z0-9-.]+$/`.

In `ch6/ts/step-1/add_developer.ts`, define a function that accepts an instance of Angular 2 control as an argument and returns `null` if the control's value is empty or matches the regular expression mentioned earlier, and `{ 'invalidEmail': true }` otherwise:

```
function validateEmail(emailControl) {
  if (!emailControl.value ||
    /^[a-zA-Z0-9_.+-]+@[a-zA-Z0-9-]+\.[a-zA-Z0-9-.]+$/.
test(emailControl.value)) {
    return null;
  } else {
    return { 'invalidEmail': true };
  }
}
```

Now, from the modules @angular/common and @angular/core import
NG_VALIDATORS and Directive, and wrap this validation function within the
following directive:

```
@Directive({
  selector: '[email-input]',
  providers: [{ provide: NG_VALIDATORS,
    useValue: validateEmail, multi: true
  }]
})
class EmailValidator {}
```

In the preceding code, we defined a single multiprovider for the token
NG_VALIDATORS. Once we inject the value associated with this token, we'll get an
array with all the validators attached to the given control (for reference, take a look
at the section for multiproviders in *Chapter 5, Dependency Injection in Angular 2*).

The only two steps left in order to make our custom validation work are to first add
the email-input attribute to the e-mail control:

```
<input id="emailInput"
    class="form-control"
    email-input
    type="text" ngControl="email"
    [(ngModel)]="developer.email"/>
```

Next, to add the directive to the list used by the component AddDeveloper
directives:

```
@Component({
  selector: 'dev-add',
  templateUrl: './add_developer.html',
  styles: [`
    input.ng-touched.ng-invalid {
      border: 1px solid red;
    }
```

```
    `],
    directives: [FORM_DIRECTIVES, EmailValidator],
    providers: [FORM_PROVIDERS]
})
class AddDeveloper {...}
```

 We're using an external template for the AddDeveloper control. There's no ultimate answer to whether a given template should be externalized or inlined within the component with templateUrl or template, respectively. The best practice states that we should inline the short templates and externalize the longer ones, but there's no specific definition as to which templates are considered short and which are long. The decision on whether the template should be used inline or put into an external file depends on the developer's personal preferences or common conventions within the organization.

Using select inputs with Angular

As the next step, we should allow the user of the application to enter the technology into which the input developer has the most proficiency. We can define a list of technologies and show them in the form as a select input.

In the AddDeveloper class, add the technologies property:

```
class AddDeveloper {
  ...
  technologies: string[] = [
    'JavaScript',
    'C',
    'C#',
    'Clojure'
  ];
  ...
}
```

Now in the template, just above the submit button, add the following markup:

```
<div class="form-group">
  <label class="control-label"
         for="technologyInput">Technology</label>
  <div>
    <select class="form-control"
            ngControl="technology" required
            [(ngModel)]="developer.technology">
```

```
      <option *ngFor="let t of technologies"
              [value]="t">{{t}}</option>
    </select>
  </div>
</div>
```

Just like for the input elements we declared earlier, Angular 2 will add the same classes depending on the state of the select input. In order to show red border around the select element when its value is invalid, we need to alter the CSS rules:

```
@Component({
  …
  styles: [
    `input.ng-touched.ng-invalid,
     select.ng-touched.ng-invalid {
       border: 1px solid red;
     }`
  ],
  …
})
class AddDeveloper {…}
```

> Notice that inlining all the styles in our components' declaration could be a bad practice, because this way, they won't be reusable. What we can do is extract all the common styles across our components into separate files. The @Component decorator has a property called styleUrls of type array where we can add a reference to the extracted styles used by the given component. This way, we can inline only the component-specific styles if required.

Right after this, we will declare the name of the control to be equal to "technology" using ngControl="technology". By using the required attribute, we will declare that the user of the application must specify the technology into which the current developer is proficient. Let's skip the [(ngModel)] attribute for the last time and see how we can define the select element's options.

Inside the select element, we will define the different options using:

```
<option *ngFor="let t of technologies"
        [value]="t">{{t}}</option>
```

This is a syntax we're already familiar with. We will simply iterate over all the technologies defined within the AddDeveloper class, and for each technology, we will show an option element with a value of the technology name.

Using the NgForm directive

We already mentioned that the form directive enhances the HTML5 form's behavior by adding some additional Angular 2-specific logic. Now, let's take a step back and take a look at the form that surrounds the input elements:

```
<form #f="ngForm" (ngSubmit)="addDeveloper()"
    class="form col-md-4" [hidden]="submitted">
  ...
</form>
```

In the preceding snippet, we defined a new identifier called f, which references to the form. We can think of the form as a composition of controls; we can access the individual controls through the form's controls property. On top of this, the form has the **touched, untouched, pristine, dirty, invalid**, and **valid** properties, which depend on the individual controls defined within the form. For example, if none of the controls within the form has been touched, then the form itself is going to be with the status untouched. However, if any of the controls in the form has been touched at least once, the form will be with the status touched as well. Similarly the form will be valid only if all its controls are valid.

In order to illustrate the usage of the form element, let's define a component with the selector control-errors, which shows the current errors for a given control. We can use it in the following way:

```
<label class="control-label" for="realNameInput">Real name</label>
<div>
  <input id="realNameInput" class="form-control" type="text"
    ngControl="realName" [(ngModel)]="developer.realName"
      required maxlength="50">
  <control-errors control="realName"
    [errors]="{
      'required': 'Real name is required',
      'maxlength': 'The maximum length of the real name is 50
characters'
      }"
  />
</div>
```

Notice that we've also added the maxlength validator to the realName control.

The control-errors element has the following properties:

- control: Declares the name of the control we want to show errors for.
- errors: Creates a mapping between control error and an error message.

Now add the following imports in `add_developer.ts`:

```
import {NgControl, NgForm} from '@angular/common';
import {Host} from '@angular/core';
```

In these imports, the `NgControl` class is the abstract class that represents the individual form components, `NgForm` represents the Angular forms, and `Host` is a parameter decorator related to the dependency injection mechanism, which we already covered in *Chapter 5, Dependency Injection in Angular 2.*

Here is a part of the component's definition:

```
@Component({
  template: '<div>{{currentError}}</div>',
  selector: 'control-errors',
  inputs: ['control', 'errors']
})
class ControlErrors {
  errors: Object;
  control: string;
  constructor(@Host() private formDir: NgForm) {}
  get currentError() {…}
}
```

The `ControlErrors` component defines two inputs: `control` — the name of the control declared with the `ngControl` directive (the value of the `ngControl` attribute) — and `errors` — the mapping between an error and an error message. They can be specified respectively by the `control` and the `errors` attributes of the `control-errors` element.

For instance, if we have control:

```
<input type="text" ngControl="foobar" required>
```

We can declare its associated `control-errors` component by using the following:

```
<control-errors control="foobar"
     [errors]="{
       'required': 'The value of foobar is required'
     }"></control-errors>
```

Inside of the `currentError` getter, in the preceding snippet, we need to do the following two things:

- Find a reference to the component declared with the `control` attribute.
- Return the error message associated with any of the errors that make the current control invalid.

Here is a snippet that implements this behavior:

```
@Component (...)
class ControlErrors {
  ...
  get currentError() {
    let control = this.formDir.controls[this.control];
    let errorsMessages = [];
    if (control && control.touched) {
      errorsMessages = Object.keys(this.errors)
        .map(k => control.hasError(k) ? this.errors[k] : null)
        .filter(error => !!error);
    }
    return errorsMessages.pop();
  }
}
```

In the first line of the implementation of currentError, we get the target control by using the controls property of the injected form. It is of the type {[key: string]: AbstractControl}, where the key is the name of the control we've declared with the ngControl directive. Once we have a reference to the instance of the target control, we can check whether its status is touched (that is, whether it has been focused), and if it is, we can loop over all the errors within the errors property of the instance of ControlError. The map function will return an array with either an error message or a null value. The only thing left is to filter all the null values and get only the error messages. Once we get the error messages for each error, we will return the last one by popping it from the errorMessages array.

The end result should look as follows:

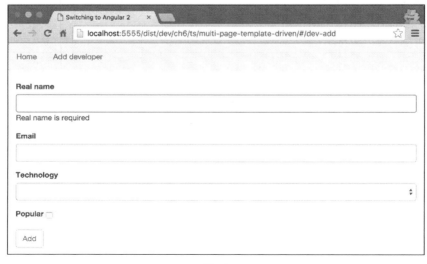

Fig. 5

If you experience any problems during the implementation of the `ControlErrors` component, you can take a look at its implementation at `ch6/ts/multi-page-template-driven/add_developer.ts`.

The `hasError` method of every control accepts as an argument an error message identifier, which is defined by the validator. For instance, in the preceding example where we defined the custom e-mail validator, we will return the following object literal when the input control has an invalid value: `{ 'invalidEmail': true }`. If we apply the `ControlErrors` component to the e-mail control, its declaration should look as follows:

```
<control-errors control="email"
[errors]="{ 'invalidEmail': 'Invalid email address' }"></control-errors>
```

Two-way data-binding with Angular 2

One of the most famous rumors about Angular 2 was that the two-way data-binding functionality was removed because of the enforced unidirectional dataflow. This is not exactly true; the Angular 2's form module implements a directive with the selector `[(ngModel)]`, which allows us to easily achieve data-binding in two directions—from the view to the model and from the model to the view.

Let's take a look at the following simple component:

```
// ch6/ts/simple-two-way-data-binding/app.ts

import {Component} from '@angular/core';
import {bootstrap} from '@angular/platform-browser-dynamic';
import {NgModel} from '@angular/common';

@Component({
  selector: 'app',
  directives: [NgModel],
  template: `
    <input type="text" [(ngModel)]="name"/>
    <div>{{name}}</div>
  `,
})
class App {
  name: string;
}

bootstrap(App, []);
```

In the preceding example, we imported the directive `NgModel` from the `@angular/common` package. Later, in the template, we set the attribute `[(ngModel)]` to the value `name`.

At first, the syntax `[(ngModel)]` might seem a little bit unusual. From *Chapter 4, Getting Started with Angular 2 Components and Directives*, we know that the syntax `(eventName)` is used for binding to events (or outputs) triggered by a given component. On the other hand, we use the syntax `[propertyName]="foobar"` to achieve one-way data-binding by setting the value of the property (or in the terminology of the Angular 2 components, the input) with the name `propertyName` to the result of the evaluation of the expression `foobar`. The syntax `NgModel` just combines both in order to achieve data-binding in two directions. That's why we can think of it more like a syntax sugar, rather than a new concept. One of the main advantages of this syntax compared to AngularJS 1.x is that we can tell which bindings are one-way and which are two-way only by looking at the template.

> Just like `(click)` has its canonical syntax `on-click` and `[propertyName]` has `bind-propertyName`, the alternative syntax of `[(ngModel)]` is `bindon-ngModel`.

If you open `http://localhost:5555/dist/dev/ch6/ts/simple-two-way-data-binding/`, you will see the following result:

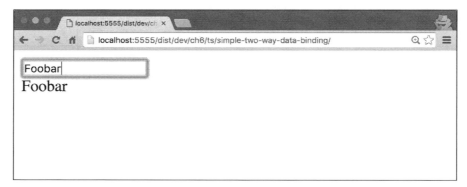

Fig. 6

Once you change the value of the input box, it will automatically update the following label.

We already used the `NgModel` directive in the preceding templates. For example, we bound to the developer's e-mail using:

```
<input id="emailInput"
       class="form-control" type="text"
       ngControl="email" [(ngModel)]="developer.email"
       email-input>
```

This way, the value of the e-mail property of the developer object attached to the `AddDeveloper` component's instance is going to be updated once we change the value of the text input.

Storing the form data

Let's peek at the interface of the `AddDeveloper` component's controller again:

```
export class AddDeveloper {
  submitted: false;
  successMessage: string;
  developer = new Developer();
  //...
  constructor(private developers: DeveloperCollection) {}
  addDeveloper(form) {...}
}
```

It has a field of the type `Developer`, and we bind the form controls to its properties using the `NgModel` directive. The class also has a method called `addDeveloper`, which is being invoked on the submission of the form. We declare this by binding to the `submit` event using:

```
<!-- ch6/ts/multi-page-template-driven/add_developer.html -->
<form #f="form" (ngSubmit)="addDeveloper()"
      class="form col-md-4" [hidden]="submitted">

  ...
  <button class="btn btn-default"
      type="submit" [disabled]="!f.form.valid">Add</button>
</form>
```

In the preceding snippet, we can notice two more things. We got a reference to the form using `#f="ngForm"` and we bound the disabled property of the button to the expression: `!f.form.valid`. We already described the `NgForm` control in the previous section; its valid property will have a value true once all the controls within the form have valid values.

Now, let's suppose we've entered valid values for all the input controls in the form. This means that its **submit** button will be enabled. Once we press *Enter* or we click on the **Add** button, the `addDeveloper` method will be invoked. The following is a sample implementation of this method:

```
class AddDeveloper {
  //...
addDeveloper() {
    this.developer.id = this.developers.getAll().length + 1;
    this.developers.addDeveloper(this.developer);
    this.successMessage = `Developer ${this.developer.realName} was
successfully added`;
    this.submitted = true;
  }
```

Initially, we set the `id` property of the current developer to equal the total number of developers in `DeveloperCollection`, plus one. Later, we added the developer to the collection and set the value of the `successMessage` property. Right after this, we set the property submitted to equal to `true`, which will result in hiding the form.

Listing all the stored developers

Now that we can add a new entry to the developers' collection, let's show a list of all the developers on the front page of the "Coders repository".

Open the file `ch6/ts/step-1/home.ts` and enter the following content:

```
import {Component} from '@angular/core';
import {DeveloperCollection} from './developer_collection';

@Component({
  selector: 'home',
  templateUrl: './home.html'
})
export class Home {
  constructor(private developers: DeveloperCollection) {}
  getDevelopers() {
    return this.developers.getAll();
  }
}
```

There is nothing new to us here. We extend the functionality of the Home component by providing an external template and implementing the `getDevelopers` method, which delegates its call to the instance of `DeveloperCollection` that is injected in the constructor.

The template itself is something that we're already familiar with as well:

```
<table class="table" *ngIf="getDevelopers().length > 0">
  <thead>
    <th>Email</th>
    <th>Real name</th>
    <th>Technology</th>
    <th>Popular</th>
  </thead>
  <tr *ngFor="let dev of getDevelopers()">
    <td>{{dev.email}}</td>
    <td>{{dev.realName}}</td>
    <td>{{dev.technology}}</td>
    <td [ngSwitch]="dev.popular">
      <span *ngSwitchCase="true">Yes</span>
      <span *ngSwitchCase="false">Not yet</span>
    </td>
  </tr>
</table>
<div *ngIf="getDevelopers().length == 0">
  There are no any developers yet
</div>
```

We list all the developers as rows within an HTML table. For each developer, we check the status of its popular flag. If its value is `true`, then for the **Popular** column, we show a span with the text `Yes`, otherwise we set the text to `No`.

When you enter a few developers in the **Add Developer** page and you navigate to the home page after that, you should see a result similar to the following screenshot:

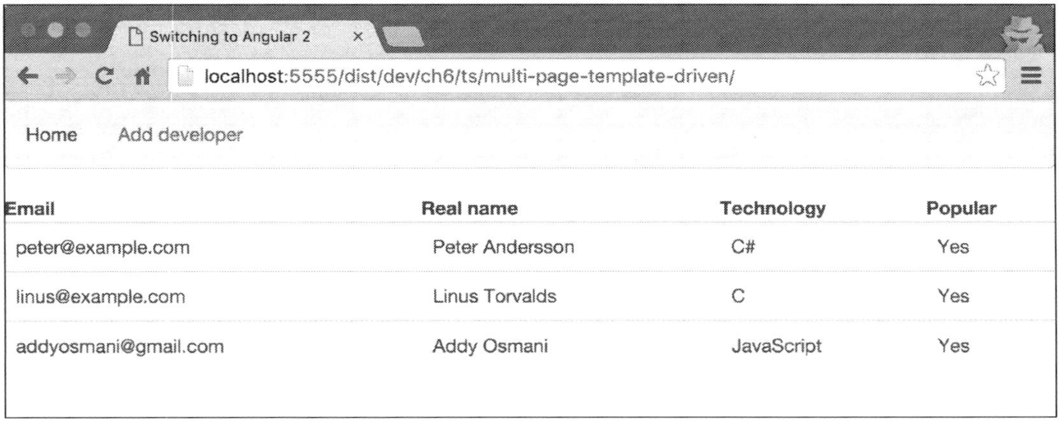
Switching to Angular 2
localhost:5555/dist/dev/ch6/ts/multi-page-template-driven/
Home
Add developer
Email
Real name
Technology
Popular
peter@example.com
Peter Andersson
C#
Yes
linus@example.com
Linus Torvalds
C
Yes
addyosmani@gmail.com
Addy Osmani
JavaScript
Yes

Fig. 7

You can find the complete functionality of the application at `ch6/ts/multi-page-template-driven`.

Summary

So far, we have explained the basics of routing in Angular 2. We took a look at how we can define different routes and implement the components associated with them that are displayed on route change. In order to link to the different routes, we explained `routerLink`, and we also used the `router-outlet` directives for pointing out where the components associated with the individual routes should be rendered.

Another thing we took a look at was the Angular 2 forms functionality with built-in and custom validation. After this, we explained the `NgModel` directive, which provides to us two-way data-binding.

In the next chapter, we will cover how we can develop model-driven forms and child and parametrized routes, use the `Http` module for making RESTful calls, and transform data with custom pipes.

7

Explaining Pipes and Communicating with RESTful Services

In the last chapter, we covered some very powerful features of the framework. However, we can go even deeper into the functionality of Angular's forms module and router. In the next sections, we'll explain how we can:

- Develop model-driven forms.
- Define parameterized routes.
- Define child routes.
- Use the Http module for communication with RESTful APIs.
- Transform data with custom pipes.

Note that the forms and router modules explained in the following sections are now deprecated. Although they will be replaced with different implementations which have different APIs, they share the same foundational idea and follow similar approach. I strongly recommend you to explore this chapter in order to get better under-standing of how these modules work.

We will explore all these concepts in the process of extending the functionality of the "Coders repository" application. At the beginning of the previous chapter, we mentioned that we're going to allow import of developers from GitHub. But before we implement this feature, let's extend the functionality of the form.

Developing model-driven forms in Angular 2

These are going to be the last steps in finishing the "Coders repository". You can build on top of the code at `ch6/ts/step-1/` (or `ch6/ts/step-2` depending on your previous work) in order to extend the application's functionality with the new concepts we're going to cover. The complete example is located at `ch7/ts/multi-page-model-driven`.

This is the result that we are going to achieve by the end of this section:

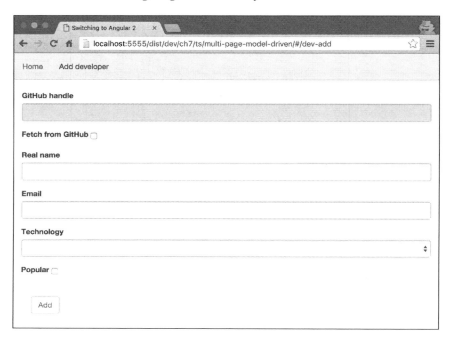

In the preceding screenshot, there are the following two forms:

- A form for importing existing users from GitHub that contains:
    - The input for the GitHub handle.
    - A checkbox that points out whether we want to import the developer from GitHub or enter it manually.
- A form for entering new users manually.

The second form looks exactly the way we finished it in the last section. However, this time, its definition looks a little bit different:

```
<form class="form col-md-4"
      [ngFormModel]="addDevForm" [hidden]="submitted">
  <!-- TODO -->
</form>
```

Notice that this time, we don't have the submit handler or the #f="ngForm" attribute. Instead, we use the [ngFormModel] attribute in order to bind to a property defined inside the component's controller. By using this attribute, we can bind to something called ControlGroup. As its name states, the ControlGroup class consists of a list of controls grouped together with the sets of validation rules associated with them.

We need to use a similar declaration to *import a developer* form. However, this time, we will provide a different value of the [ngFormModel] attribute, since we are going to define a different control group in the component's controller. Place the following snippet above the form we introduced earlier:

```
<form class="form col-md-4"
    [ngFormModel]="importDevForm" [hidden]="submitted">
<!-- TODO -->
</form>
```

Now, let's declare the importDevForm and addDevForm properties in the component's controller:

```
import {ControlGroup} from '@angular/common';
@Component(...)
export class AddDeveloper {
  importDevForm: ControlGroup;
  addDevForm: ControlGroup;
  ...
  constructor(private developers: DeveloperCollection,
    fb: FormBuilder) {...}
  addDeveloper() {...}
}
```

Initially, we imported the ControlGroup class from the @angular/common module and, later, declared the required properties in the controller. Let's also notice that we have one additional parameter of the constructor of AddDeveloper called fb of the type FormBuilder.

`FormBuilder` provides a programmable API for the definition of `ControlGroups` where we can attach validation behavior to each control in the group. Let's use the `FormBulder` instance for the initialization of the `importDevForm` and `addDevForm` properties:

```
...
constructor(private developers: DeveloperCollection,
  fb: FormBuilder) {
  this.importDevForm = fb.group({
    githubHandle: ['', Validators.required],
    fetchFromGitHub: [false]
  });
  this.addDevForm = fb.group({
    realName: ['', Validators.required],
    email: ['', validateEmail],
    technology: ['', Validators.required],
    popular: [false]
  });
}
...
```

The `FormBuilder` instance has a method called `group` that allows us to define properties, such as the default values and the validators for the individual controls in a given form.

According to the preceding snippet, `importDevForm` has two fields that we introduced earlier: `githubHandle` and `fetchFromGitHub`. We declared that the value of the `githubHandle` control is required and set the default value of the control `fetchFromGitHub` to `false`.

In the second form, `addDevForm`, we declare four controls. For the `realName` control as the default value, we set the empty string and use `Validators.requred` in order to introduce validation behavior (which is exactly what we did for the `githubHandle` control). As a validator for the e-mail input, we will use the `validateEmail` function and set its initial value to an empty string. The `validateEmail` function used for validation is the one we defined in the previous chapter:

```
function validateEmail(emailControl) {
  if (!emailControl.value ||
      /^[a-zA-Z0-9_.+-]+@[a-zA-Z0-9-]+\.[a-zA-Z0-9-.]+$/.
test(emailControl.value)) {
    return null;
  } else {
    return { 'invalidEmail': true };
  }
}
```

The last two controls we define here are the `technology` control, which value is required and has an empty string as its initial value, and the `popular` control with its initial value set to `false`.

Using composition of control validators

We took a look at how we can apply a single validator to form controls. However, in some applications, the domain may require more complex validation logic. For example, if we want to apply both the required and the `validateEmail` validators to the e-mail control, we should do the following:

```
this.addDevForm = fb.group({
  ...
  email: ['', Validators.compose([
    Validators.required,
    validateEmail]
  )],
  ...
});
```

The `compose` method of the `Validators` object accepts as an argument an array of validators and returns a new validator. The new validator's behavior is going to be a composition of the logic defined in the individual validators passed as an argument, and they are going to be applied in the same order as they were introduced in the array.

The property names in the object literal passed to the `group` method should match with the values that we set to the `ngControl` attributes of the inputs in the template.

This is the complete template of `importDevForm`:

```
<form class="form col-md-4"
    [ngFormModel]="importDevForm" [hidden]="submitted" >
  <div class="form-group">
    <label class="control-label"
          for="githubHandleInput">GitHub handle</label>
    <div>
      <input id="githubHandleInput"
            class="form-control" type="text"
            [disabled]="!fetchFromGitHub"
            ngControl="githubHandle">
      <control-errors control="githubHandle"
        [errors]="{
```

```
                    'required': 'The GitHub handle is required'
                }"></control-errors>
        </div>
    </div>
    <div class="form-group">
        <label class="control-label"
                for="fetchFromGitHubCheckbox">
            Fetch from GitHub
        </label>
        <input class="checkbox-inline" id="fetchFromGitHubCheckbox"
                type="checkbox" ngControl="fetchFromGitHub"
                [(ngModel)]="fetchFromGitHub">
    </div>
</form>
```

In the preceding template, you can notice that once the flag submitted has the value `true`, so the form will be hidden from the user. Next to the first input element, we set the value of the `ngControl` attribute to `githubHandle`.

 Note that the value of the `ngControl` attribute of the given input element must match the name we used for its corresponding control declaration in the definition of `ControlGroup` within the component's controller.

With regard to the `githubHandle` control, we also set the disabled attribute to equal the result of the evaluation of the expression: `!fetchFromGitHub`. This way, when the `fetchFromGitHub` checkbox is unchecked, the `githubHandle` control will be disabled. Similarly, in case of the example in the previous sections, we used the `ControlErrors` component we defined previously. This time, we set a single error with the message **The GitHub handle is required**.

The markup for the form `addDevForm` looks quite similar, so we won't describe it in detail here. If you're not completely sure of how to approach developing it, you can take a look at the complete implementation at `ch7/ts/multi-page-model-driven/ add_developer.html`.

The last part of the template we're going to take a look at is the `Submit` button:

```
<button class="btn btn-default"
        (click)="addDeveloper()"
        [disabled]="(fetchFromGitHub && !importDevForm.valid) ||
                    (!fetchFromGitHub && !addDevForm.valid)">
    Add
</button>
```

Clicking on the button will invoke the `addDeveloper` method defined in the component's controller. In the expression set as value of the `[disabled]` attribute, we initially check which form is selected by using the value of the property bound to the checkbox, that is, we verify whether the user wants to add a new developer or import an existing one from GitHub. If the first option is selected (that is, if the checkbox is not checked), we verify whether the `ControlGroup` for adding a new developer is valid. If it is valid, then the button will be enabled, otherwise it will be disabled. We will do the same in cases when the user has checked the checkbox for importing a developer from GitHub.

Exploring the HTTP module of Angular

Now, after we develop the forms for both importing existing and adding new developers, it is the time to implement the logic behind it in the controller of the component.

For this purpose, we need to communicate with the GitHub API. Although we can do this directly from the component's controller, by doing it this way, we can couple it with the RESTful API of GitHub. In order to enforce further separation of concerns, we can extract the logic for communication with GitHub into a separate service called `GitHubGateway`. Open a file called `github_gateway.ts` and enter the following content:

```
import {Injectable} from '@angular/core';
import {Http} from '@angular/http';

@Injectable()
export class GitHubGateway {
  constructor(private http: Http) {}
  getUser(username: string) {
    return this.http
    .get(`https://api.github.com/users/${username}`);
  }
}
```

Initially, we imported the `Http` class from the `@angular/http` module. All the HTTP-related functionality is externalized and is outside the Angular's core. Since `GitHubGateway` accepts a dependency, which needs to be injected through the DI mechanism of the framework, we will decorate it with the `@Injectable` decorator.

The only functionality from the GitHub's API we're going to use is the one for fetching users, so we will define a single method called `getUser`. As an argument, it accepts the GitHub handle of the developer.

Note that if you make more than 60 requests per day to the GitHub's API, you might get the error **GitHub API Rate limit exceeded**. This is due to the rate limits for requests without a GitHub API token. For further information, visit `https://github.com/blog/1509-personal-api-tokens`.

Inside the `getUser` method, we use the instance of the `Http` service that we've received in the `constructor` function. The `Http` service's API stays as close to the HTML5 fetch API as possible. However, there are a couple of differences. The most significant one of them is that at the moment of writing this content, all the methods of the `Http` instances return `Observables` instead of `Promises`.

The `Http` service instances have the following API:

- `request(url: string | Request, options: RequestOptionsArgs)`: Makes a request to the specified URL. The request can be configured using `RequestOptionsArgs`:

```
http.request('http://example.com/', {
  method: 'get',
  search: 'foo=bar',
  headers: new Headers({
    'X-Custom-Header': 'Hello'
  })
});
```

- `get(url: string, options?: RequestOptionsArgs)`: Makes a get request to the specified URL. The request headers and other options can be configured using the second argument.

- `post(url: string, options?: RequestOptionsArgs)`: Makes a post request to the specified URL. The request body, headers, and other options can be configured using the second argument.

- `put(url: string, options?: RequestOptionsArgs)`: Makes a put request to the specified URL. The request headers and other options can be configured using the second argument.

- `patch(url: string, options?: RequestOptionsArgs)`: Makes a patch request to the specified URL. The request headers and other options can be configured using the second argument.

- `delete(url: string, options?: RequestOptionsArgs)`: Makes a delete request to the specified URL. The request headers and other options can be configured using the second argument.

- `head(url: string, options?: RequestOptionsArgs)`: Makes a head request to the specified URL. The request headers and other options can be configured using the second argument.

Using Angular's HTTP module

Now, let's implement the logic for importing existing users from GitHub! Open the file `ch6/ts/step-2/add_developer.ts` and enter the following imports:

```
import {Response, HTTP_PROVIDERS} from '@angular/http';
import {GitHubGateway} from './github_gateway';
```

Add `HTTP_PROVIDERS` and `GitHubGateway` to the list of providers of the `AddDeveloper` component:

```
@Component({
  ...
  providers: [GitHubGateway, FORM_PROVIDERS, HTTP_PROVIDERS]
})
class AddDeveloper {...}
```

As the next step, we have to include the following parameters in the constructor of the class:

```
constructor(private githubAPI: GitHubGateway,
  private developers: DeveloperCollection,
  fb: FormBuilder) {
  //...
}
```

This way, the `AddDeveloper` class' instances will have a private property called `githubAPI`.

The only thing left is to implement the `addDeveloper` method and allow the user to import existing developers by using the `GitHubGateway` instance.

Once the user presses the **Add** button, we need to check whether we need to import an existing GitHub user or add a new developer. For this purpose, we can use the value of the `fetchFromGitHub` control:

```
if (this.importDevForm.controls['fetchFromGitHub'].value) {
  // Import developer
} else {
  // Add new developer
}
```

If it has a truthy value, then we can invoke the `getUser` method of the `githubAPI` property and pass the value of the `githubHandle` control as an argument:

```
this.githubAPI.getUser(model.githubHandle)
```

In the `getUser` method, we delegate the call to the `Http` service's `get` method, which returns an observable. In order to get the result that the observable is going to push, we need to pass a callback to its `subscribe` method:

```
this.githubAPI.getUser(model.githubHandle)
  .map((r: Response) => r.json())
  .subscribe((res: any) => {
    // "res" contains the response of the GitHub's API
  });
```

In the preceding snippet, we first establish the HTTP `get` request. After this, we'll get the observable that, in general cases, will emit a series of values (in this case, only a single one—the response of the request) and map them to the JSON representation of their bodies. If the response fails or its body is not a valid JSON string, then we will get an error.

> Note that in order to reduce the size of RxJS, Angular's core team has included only its core. In order to use the methods map and catch, you need to add the following imports at add_developer.ts:
>
> **import 'rxjs/add/operator/map';**
>
> **import 'rxjs/add/operator/catch';**

Now let's implement the body of the subscribe callback:

```
let dev = new Developer();
dev.githubHandle = res.login;
dev.email = res.email;
dev.popular = res.followers >= 1000;
dev.realName = res.name;
dev.id = res.id;
dev.avatarUrl = res.avatar_url;
this.developers.addDeveloper(dev);
this.successMessage = `Developer ${dev.githubHandle} successfully
imported from GitHub`;
```

In the preceding example, we set the properties of a new `Developer` instance. Here, we established the mapping between the object returned from GitHub's API and the developer's representation in our application. We also considered a developer as popular if she or he has above 1,000 followers.

The entire implementation of the `addDeveloper` method can be found at `ch7/ts/multi-page-model-driven/add_developer.ts`.

> In order to handle failed requests, we can use the `catch` method of the observable instances:
> ```
> this.githubAPI.getUser(model.githubHandle)
> .catch((error, source, caught) => {
>   console.log(error)
>   return error;
> })
> ```

Defining parameterized views

As the next step, let's dedicate a special page for each developer. Inside of it, we'll be able to take a detailed look at his or her profile. Once the user clicks on the name of any of the developers on the home page of the application, he or she should be redirected to a page with a detailed profile of the selected developer. The end result will look as follows:

In order to do this, we need to pass an identifier of the developer to the component that shows developer's detailed profile. Open `app.ts` and add the following import:

```
import {DeveloperDetails} from './developer_details';
```

We haven't developed the `DeveloperDetails` component yet, so if you run the application, you will get an error. We will define the component in the next paragraph, but before this, let's alter the `@RouteConfig` definition of the `App` component:

```
@RouteConfig([
  //...
  new Route({
    component: DeveloperDetails,
    name: 'DeveloperDetails',
    path: '/dev-details/:id/...'
  }),
  //...
])
class App {}
```

We added a single route with the `DeveloperDetails` component associated with it, and as an alias, we used the string `"DeveloperDetails"`.

The value of the `component` property is a reference to the constructor of the component, which should handle the given route. Once the source code of the application gets minified for production, the component name may differ from the one we've entered. This will create problems when referencing the route within the templates using the `routerLink` directive. In order to prevent this from happening, the core team introduced the `name` property that, in this case, equals to the name of the controller.

> Although in all the examples so far, we set the alias of the route to be the same as the name of the component's controller, this is not required. This convention is used for simplicity, since it could be confusing to introduce two names: one for pointing to the route and another one for the controller associated with the given route.

In the `path` property, we declare that the route has a single parameter called `id`, and with `"..."`, we hint the framework that this route will have nested routes inside of it.

Now, let's pass the `id` of the current developer as a parameter to the `routerLink` directive. Open `home.html` in your working directory and replace the table cell where we display the developer's `realName` property with the following content:

```
<td>
  <a [routerLink]="['/DeveloperDetails',
      { 'id': dev.id }, 'DeveloperBasicInfo']">
```

```
      {{dev.realName}}
    </a>
  </td>
```

The value of the `routerLink` directive is an array with the following three elements:

- `'/DeveloperDetails'`: A string that shows the root route
- `{ 'id': dev.id }`: An object literal that declares the route parameters
- `'DeveloperBasicInfo'`: The name of a route that shows which component within the nested route in the component with the alias `DeveloperDetails` should be rendered

Defining nested routes

Now let's jump to the `DeveloperDetails` definition. In your working directory, create a file called `developer_details.ts` and enter the following content:

```
import {Component} from '@angular/core';
import {
  ROUTER_DIRECTIVES,
  RouteConfig,
  RouteParams
} from '@angular/router-deprecated';
import {Developer} from './developer';
import {DeveloperCollection} from './developer_collection';

@Component({
  selector: 'dev-details',
  template: `...`,
})
@RouteConfig(...)
export class DeveloperDetails {
  public dev: Developer;
  constructor(routeParams: RouteParams,
    developers: DeveloperCollection) {
    this.dev = developers.getUserById(
      parseInt(routeParams.params['id'])
    );
  }
}
```

In the preceding snippet, we defined a component with controller called
DeveloperDetails. You can notice that within the controller's constructor, through
the DI mechanism of Angular 2, we injected a parameter associated with the
RouteParams token. The injected parameter provides us access to the parameters
visible by the current route. We can access them using the params property of the
injected object and access the target parameter using its name as a key.

Since the parameter we got from routeParams.params['id'] is a string, we need
to parse it to a number in order to get the developer associated with the given route.
Now let's define the routes associated with DeveloperDetails:

```
@Component (...)
@RouteConfig ([{
 component: DeveloperBasicInfo,
 name: 'DeveloperBasicInfo',
 path: '/'
},
{
 component: DeveloperAdvancedInfo,
 name: 'DeveloperAdvancedInfo',
 path: '/dev-details-advanced'
}])
export class DeveloperDetails {...}
```

In the preceding snippet, there is nothing new for us. The route definition follows the
exact same rules we're already familiar with.

Now, to the template of the component, let's add links associated with the individual
nested routes:

```
@Component ({
  selector: 'dev-details',
  directives: [ROUTER_DIRECTIVES],
  template: `
    <section class="col-md-4">
      <ul class="nav nav-tabs">
        <li>
          <a [routerLink]="['./DeveloperBasicInfo']">
            Basic profile
          </a>
        </li>
        <li>
          <a [routerLink]="['./DeveloperAdvancedInfo']">
            Advanced details
          </a>
```

```
          </li>
        </ul>
        <router-outlet/>
      </section>
    `,
})
@RouteConfig(...)
export class DeveloperDetails {...}
```

Within the template, we declare two relative to the current path links. The first one points to `DeveloperBaiscInfo`, which is the name of the first route defined within `@RouteConfig` of the `DeveloperDetails` component, and respectively, the second one points to `DeveloperAdvancedInfo`.

Since the implementations of both the components are quite similar, let's take a look only at `DeveloperBasicInfo`. As an exercise, you can develop the second one or take a look at its implementation at `ch7/ts/multi-page-model-driven/developer_advanced_info.ts`:

```
import {
  Component,
  Inject,
  forwardRef,
  Host
} from '@angular/core';
import {DeveloperDetails} from './developer_details';
import {Developer} from './developer';

@Component({
  selector: 'dev-details-basic',
  styles: [...],
  template: `
    <h2>{{dev.realName}}</h2>
    <img *ngIf="dev.avatarUrl == null"
      class="avatar" src="./gravatar-60-grey.jpg" width="150">
    <img *ngIf="dev.avatarUrl != null"
      class="avatar" [src]="dev.avatarUrl" width="150">
  `
})
export class DeveloperBasicInfo {
  dev: Developer;
  constructor(@Inject(forwardRef(() => DeveloperDetails))
    @Host() parent: DeveloperDetails) {
    this.dev = parent.dev;
  }
}
```

In the preceding snippet, we injected the parent component combining the `@Inject` parameter decorator with `@Host`. Inside of `@Inject`, we use `forwardRef`, since we have a circular dependency between the packages `developer_basic_info` and `developer_details` (inside `developer_basic_info`, we import `developer_details`, and within `developer_details`, we import `developer_basic_info`).

We need a reference to the instance of the parent component in order to get the instance of the current developer corresponding to the selected route.

Transforming data with pipes

It is time for the last building block that Angular 2 provides for the development of applications that we haven't covered in detail yet—the pipes.

Just like the filters in AngularJS 1.x, pipes are intended to encapsulate all the data-transformation logic. Let's take a look at the template of the home page of the application we just developed:

```
...
<td [ngSwitch]="dev.popular">
  <span *ngSwitch-when="true">Yes</span>
  <span *ngSwitch-when="false">Not yet</span>
</td>
...
```

In the preceding snippet, depending on the value of the `popular` property, we showed different data using the `NgSwitch` and `NgSwitchThen` directives. Although this works, it is redundant.

Developing stateless pipes

Let's develop a pipe that transforms the value of the `popular` property and uses it in the place of `NgSwitch` and `NgSwitchThen`. The pipe will accept three arguments: a value that should be transformed, a string that should be displayed when the value is truthy, and another string that should be displayed in case of a falsy value.

With the use of an Angular 2 custom pipe, we will be able to simplify the template to:

```
<td>{{dev.popular | boolean: 'Yes': 'No'}}</td>
```

We could even use emojis:

```
<td>{{dev.popular | boolean: '👍': '👎'}}</td>
```

We apply the pipe to the value the same way we do in AngularJS 1.x. The arguments we pass to the pipe should be separated by the colon (:) symbol.

In order to develop an Angular 2 pipe, we need the following imports:

```
import {Pipe, PipeTransform} from '@angular/core';
```

The `Pipe` decorator can be used for adding metadata to the class that implements the data transformation logic. The `PipeTransform` is an interface with a single method called transform:

```
import {Pipe, PipeTransform} from '@angular/core';

@Pipe({
  name: 'boolean'
})
export class BooleanPipe implements PipeTransform {
  constructor() {}
  transform(flag: boolean, args: string[]): string {
    return flag ? args[0] : args[1];
  }
}
```

The preceding snippet is the entire implementation of `BooleanPipe`. The name of the pipe determines the way it should be used in templates.

The last thing we need to do before being able to use the pipe is to add the `BooleanPipe` class to the list of pipes used by the `Home` component (`BooleanPipe` already holds the metadata attached to it by the `@Pipe` decorator, so its name is attached to it):

```
@Component({
  ...
  pipes: [BooleanPipe],
})
export class Home {
  constructor(private developers: DeveloperCollection) {}
  getDevelopers() {...}
}
```

Using Angular's built-in pipes

Angular 2 provides the following set of built-in pipes:

- `CurrencyPipe`: This pipe is used for formatting currency data. As an argument, it accepts the abbreviation of the currency type (that is, `"EUR"`, `"USD"`, and so on). It can be used in the following way:

  `{{ currencyValue | currency: 'USD' }} <!-- USD42 -->`

- `DatePipe`: This pipe is used for the transformation of dates. It can be used in the following way:

  `{{ dateValue | date: 'shortTime'  }} <!-- 12:00 AM -->`

- `DecimalPipe`: This pipe is used for transformation of decimal numbers. The argument it accepts is of the following form: `"{minIntegerDigits}.{minFractionDigits}-{maxFractionDigits}"`. It can be used in the following way:

  `{{ 42.1618 | number: '3.1-2' }} <!-- 042.16 -->`

- `JsonPipe`: This transforms a JavaScript object into a JSON string. It can be used in the following way:

  `{{ { foo: 42 } | json }} <!-- { "foo": 42 } -->`

- `LowerCasePipe`: This transforms a string to lowercase. It can be used in the following way:

  `{{ FOO | lowercase }} <!-- foo -->`

- `UpperCasePipe`: This transforms a string to uppercase. It can be used in the following way:

  `{{ 'foo' | uppercase }} <!-- FOO -->`

- `PercentPipe`: This transforms a number into a percentage. It can be used in the following way:

  `{{ 42 | percent: '2.1-2' }}  <!-- 4,200.0% -->`

- `SlicePipe`: This returns a slice of an array. The pipe accepts the start and the end indexes of the slice. It can be used in the following way:

  `{{ [1, 2, 3] | slice: 1: 2 }} <!-- 2 -->`

- `AsyncPipe`: This is a `stateful` pipe that accepts an observable or a promise. We're going to take a look at it at the end of the chapter.

Developing stateful pipes

There was one common thing between all the pipes mentioned earlier—all of them return exactly the same result each time we apply them to the same value and pass them the same set of arguments. Such pipes that hold the referentially transparency property are called pure pipes.

The `@Pipe` decorator accepts an object literal of the following type: `{ name: string, pure?: boolean }`, where the default value for the `pure` property is `true`. This means that when we decorate a given class using the `@Pipe` decorator, we can declare whether we want the pipe it implements the logic for to be either stateful or stateless. The pure property is important, because in case the pipe is stateless (that is, it returns the same result in case it is applied over the same value with the same set of arguments), the change detection can be optimized.

Now let's build a stateful pipe! Our pipe will make an HTTP `get` request to a JSON API. For this purpose, we will use the `@angular/http` module.

 Note that having business logic in a pipe is not considered as a best practice. This type of logic should be extracted into a service. The example here is for learning purposes only.

In this case, the pipe needs to hold a different state depending on the status of the request (that is, whether it is pending or completed). We will use the pipe in the following way:

```
{{ "http://example.com/user.json" | fetchJson | json }}
```

This way, we apply the `fetchJson` pipe over the URL, and once we have response from the remote service and the promise for the request has been resolved, we can apply the `json` pipe over the object we got from the response. The example also shows how we can chain pipes with Angular 2.

Similarly, in case of the previous example, for the development of a stateless pipe, we have to import `Pipe` and `PipeTransform`. However, this time, because of the HTTP request functionality, we also need to import the `Http` and `Response` classes from the `'@angular/http'` module:

```
import {Pipe, PipeTransform} from '@angular/core';
import {Http, Response} from '@angular/http';
import 'rxjs/add/operator/toPromise';
```

Each time it happens to apply the `fetchJson` pipe to a different argument compared to the one we got in the previous invocation, we need to make a new HTTP `get` request. This means that as the state of the pipe, we need to keep at least the values of the response of the remote service and the last URL:

```
@Pipe({
  name: 'fetchJson',
  pure: false
})
export class FetchJsonPipe implements PipeTransform {
  private data: any;
  private prevUrl: string;
  constructor(private http: Http) {}
  transform(url: string): any {…}
}
```

The only piece of logic left is the `transform` method:

```
…
transform(url: string): any {
  if (this.prevUrl !== url) {
    this.http.get(url).toPromise(Promise)
      .then((data: Response) => data.json())
      .then(result => this.data = result);
    this.prevUrl = url;
  }
  return this.data || {};
}
…
```

Inside of it, we initially compared the URL passed as an argument with the one we currently keep a reference to. If they are different, we initiate a new HTTP `get` request using the local instance of the `Http` class, which was passed to the `constructor` function. Once the request is completed, we parse the response to JSON and set the `data` property to the result.

Now, let's suppose the pipe has started an `Http get` request, and before it is completed, the change detection mechanism invokes the pipe again. In this case, we will compare the `prevUrl` property with the `url` parameter. In case they are the same, we won't perform a new `http` request, and we will immediately return the value of the `data` property. In case `prevUrl` has a different value from `url`, we will start a new request.

Using stateful pipes

Now let's use the pipe that we developed! The application that we are going to implement provides to the user a text input and a button. Once the user enters a value in the text input and presses the button, below the text input will appear the avatar corresponding to the GitHub user, as shown in the following screenshot:

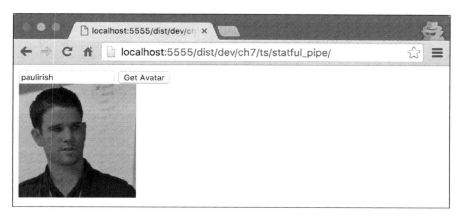

Now, let's develop a sample component, which will allow us to enter the GitHub user's handle:

```
// ch7/ts/statful_pipe/app.ts

@Component({
  selector: 'app',
  providers: [HTTP_PROVIDERS],
  pipes: [FetchJsonPipe, ObjectGetPipe],
  template: `
    <input type="text" #input>
    <button (click)=" setUsername(input.value)">Get Avatar</button>
  `
})
class App {
  username: string;
  setUsername(user: string) {
    this.username = user;
  }
}
```

In the preceding example, we added `FetchJsonPipe` used by the `App` component. The only thing left is to show the GitHub avatar of the user. We can easily achieve this by altering the template of the preceding component with the following `img` declaration:

```
<img width="160" [src]="(('https://api.github.com/users/' + username)
| fetchJson).avatar_url">
```

Initially, we appended the GitHub handle to the base URL used for fetching users from the API. Later, we applied the `fetchJson` filter over it, and from the returned result, we got the `avatar_url` property.

 Although the previous example works, it is unnatural to have business logic in your pipes. It will be far better to implement the logic for communication with the GitHub's API into a service or, at least, invoke the `get` method of the instance of the `Http` class in a component.

Using Angular's AsyncPipe

Angular's `AsyncPipe` transform method accepts as an argument an observable or a promise. Once the argument pushes a value (that is, the promise has been resolved or the `subscribe` callback of the observable is invoked with a value), `AsyncPipe` will return it as a result. Let's take a look at the following example:

```
// ch7/ts/async-pipe/app.ts
@Component({
  selector: 'greeting',
  template: 'Hello {{ greetingPromise | async }}'
})
class Greeting {
  greetingPromise = new Promise<string>(resolve => this.resolve =
resolve);
  resolve: Function;
  constructor() {
    setTimeout(_ => {
      this.resolve('Foobar!');
    }, 3000);
  }
}
```

Here, we defined an Angular 2 component, which has two properties: `greetingPromise` of the type `Promise<string>` and `resolve` of the type `Function`. We initialized the `greetingPromise` property with a new `Promise<string>` instance, and as value of the `resolve` property, we set the `resolve` callback of the promise.

In the constructor of the class, we start a timeout with the duration of 3,000 ms, and inside of its callback, we resolve the promise. Once the promise is resolved, the value of the expression `{{ greetingPromise | async }}` will be evaluated to the string `Foobar!`. The end result that the user will see on the screen is the text **Hello Foobar!**.

The `async` pipe is extremely powerful when we combine it with an `Http` request or together with an observable, which pushes a sequence of values.

Using AsyncPipe with observables

We're already familiar with the concept of observables from the previous chapters. We can say that an observable object allows us to subscribe to the emission of a sequence of values, for instance:

```
let observer = new Observable<number>(observer => {
  setInterval(() => {
    observer.next(new Date().getTime());
  }, 1000);
});
observer.subscribe(date => console.log(date));
```

Once we subscribe to the observable, it will start emitting values each second, which are going to be printed in the console. Let's combine this snippet with the component's definition and implement a simple timer:

```
// ch7/ts/async-pipe/app.ts
@Component({
  selector: 'timer'
})
class Timer {
  username: string;
  timer: Observable<number>;
  constructor() {
    let counter = 0;
    this.timer = new Observable<number>(observer => {
```

```
        setInterval(() => {
          observer.next(new Date().getTime());
        }, 1000);
      });
    }
  }
```

The only thing left in order to be able to use the timer component is to add its template. We can subscribe to the observable directly in our template by using the `async` pipe:

```
{{ timer | async | date: "medium" }}
```

This way, each second we will get the new value emitted by the observable, and the `date` pipe will transform it into a readable form.

Summary

In this chapter, we took a deep dive into the Angular 2 forms by developing a model-driven one and combining it with the `http` module in order to be able to add developers to our repository. We took a look at some advanced features of the new component-based router and saw how we can use and develop our customized stateful and stateless pipes.

The next chapter will be dedicated to how we can make our Angular 2 applications SEO-friendly by taking advantage of the server-side rendering that the module universal provides. We will also take a look at angular-cli and the other tools that make our experience as developers better.

8
Development Experience and Server-Side Rendering

We are already familiar with all the core concepts of Angular 2. We know how to develop a component-based user interface, taking advantage of all the building blocks that the framework provides—directives, components, dependency injections, pipes, forms, and the brand new component-based router.

For the next step, we'll look at where to begin when we want to build a **single-page application (SPA)** from scratch. This chapter describes how to do the following:

- Use Web Workers for performance-sensitive applications.
- Build SEO-friendly applications with server-side rendering.
- Bootstrap a project as quickly as possible.
- Enhance our experience as developers.

So, let's begin!

Running applications in Web Workers

When talking about performance in the context of frontend web development, we can either mean network, computational, or rendering performance. In this section, we'll concentrate on rendering and computational performance.

First, let's make a parallel between a web application and a video, and between a browser and a video player. The biggest difference between the web application running in the browser and the video file playing in the video player is that the web page needs to be generated dynamically, in contrast to the video which has been recorded, encoded, and distributed. However, in both the cases, the user of the application sees a sequence of frames; the core difference is how these frames are being generated. In the world of video processing, when we play a video, we have it already recorded; it is the responsibility of the video decoder to extract the individual frames based on the compression algorithm. In contrast to this, on the Web, JavaScript, and CSS are in charge of producing frames, rendered by the browser's rendering engine.

In the context of the browser, we can think of each frame as a snapshot of the web page at a given moment. The different frames are rendered fast one after another, so in theory, the end user of the application should see them smoothly incorporated together, just like a video played in a video player.

On the Web, we are trying to reach 60 fps (frames per second), which means that each frame has about 16 ms to be computed and rendered on the screen. This duration includes the time required by the browser to make all the necessary calculations for the layout and the rendering of the page, and also the time that our JavaScript needs to execute.

In the end, we have less than 16 ms (because of the browser rendering functionality that takes time depending on the calculations it needs to perform) for our JavaScript to finish execution. If it doesn't fit in this duration, the frame rate will drop by half. Since JavaScript is a single-threaded language, all the calculations need to happen in the main UI thread that, in the case of computationally-intensive applications (such as image or video processing, marshaling and unmarshaling big JSON strings, and so on), can lead to very poor user experience because of the frames being dropped.

HTML5 introduced an API called **Web Workers**, which allows the execution of client-side code in the browser environment into multiple threads. For simplicity, the standard doesn't allow shared memory between individual threads, but instead allows communication with message passing. The messages exchanged between Web Workers and the main UI thread must be strings, which often requires the serialization and deserialization of JSON strings.

The lack of shared memory between the individual workers, and the workers and the main UI thread brings a couple of limitations, such as:

- Disabled access to the DOM by the worker threads.
- Global variables cannot be shared among the individual computational units (that is, worker threads and main UI threads and vice versa).

Web Workers and Angular 2

Because of the platform agnostic design of Angular 2, the core team decided to take advantage of this API, and during the summer of 2015, Google embedded Web Workers support into the framework. This feature allows most of the Angular 2 applications to be run on a separate thread, making the main UI thread responsible only for rendering. This helps us achieve the goal of 60 fps much easily than running the entire application in a single thread.

The Web Workers support is not enabled by default. When enabling it, we need to keep something in mind—in a Web Workers-ready application, the components are not going to be run in the main UI thread, which does not allow us to directly manipulate the DOM. In this case, we need to use bindings, such as inputs, outputs, and a combination of both with `NgModel`.

Bootstrapping an application running in Web Worker

Let's make the to-do application that we developed in *Chapter 4, Getting Started with Angular 2 Components and Directives* work in Web Workers. You can find the example that we'll explore at `ch8/ts/todo_webworkers/`.

First of all, let's discuss the changes that we need to make. Take a look at `ch4/ts/inputs-outputs/app.ts`. Notice that inside of `app.ts`, we included the `bootstrap` function from the `@angular/platform-browser-dynamic` module. This is the first thing we need to modify! The bootstrap process of an application running in a background process is different.

Before refactoring our code, let's take a look at a diagram that illustrates the `bootstrap` process of a typical Angular 2 application running in Web Workers:

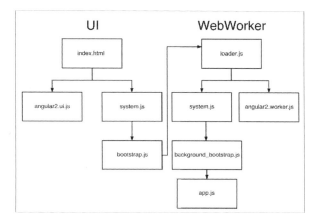

Jason Teplitz, who implemented the Web Worker support in Angular 2, presented this diagram during his talk on *AngularConnect 2015*.

The diagram has two parts: **UI** and **Web Worker**. UI shows the actions performed during initialization in the main UI thread; the **Web Worker** part of the diagram shows how the application gets bootstrapped in the background thread. Now, let's explain the bootstrap process step by step.

First, the user opens the `index.html` page, which triggers the download of the following two files:

- The UI bundle of Angular 2 used for applications running in Web Worker.
- The `system.js` bundle (we talked about the global object System in *Chapter 3, TypeScript Crash Course*. We can think of the `system.js` bundle as a polyfill for the module loader).

Using `system.js`, we download the script used for the initialization of the part of the application running in the main UI thread. This script starts `loader.js` in Web Worker. This is the first script that is running in a background thread. Once the worker is started, `loader.js` will download `system.js` and the bundle of Angular 2, which is meant to be run in the background thread. The first request will usually hit the cache because `system.js` is already requested by the main thread. Using the module loader, we download the script that is responsible for bootstrapping the background app `background_bootstrap.js`, which will finally start the functionality of our application in the background.

From now on, the entire application that we built will be run in Web Worker and will exchange messages with the main UI thread for responding to user events and rendering instructions.

Now that we are aware of the basic flow of events during initialization when using workers, let's refactor our to-do application to take advantage of them.

Migrating an application to Web Worker

Inside of `index.html`, we need to add the following scripts:

```
<!-- ch8/ts/todo_webworkers/index.html -->
...
<script src="/node_modules/systemjs/dist/system.src.js">
</script>
<script src="/node_modules/reflect-metadata/Reflect.js"></script>
<script src="/node_modules/zone.js/dist/zone.js">
</script>
```

```
<!--
   Contains some basic SystemJS configuration in order to
   allow us to load Angular
-->
<script src="./config.js"></script>
<script>
System.import('./bootstrap.js')
   .catch(function () {
      console.log('Report this error to https://github.com/mgechev/
switching-to-angular2/issues', e);
   });
</script>
...
```

In the preceding snippet, we've included references to `system.js`, `zone.js` and `reflect-metadata`.

Right after this, we configure `system.js` by setting the `baseURL` property of the module loader, which happens in `config.js`. For the next step, we will explicitly import the `bootstrap.js` file, which contains the logic used for starting the `loader.js` script in Web Worker.

Let's explore `bootstrap.js`, which is the original of the transpiled `bootstrap.js`:

```
// ch8/ts/todo_webworkers/bootstrap.ts
import {bootstrapWorkerUi} from '@angular/platform-browser-dynamic';

bootstrapWorkerUi('loader.js');
```

We pass `'loader.js'` to the invocation of `bootstrapWorkerUi`. This way Angular knows that loader.js is going to run in a background thread. The script is located in the application's root.

Now, we can move to the right of the diagram given in the *Bootstrapping an application running in a Web Worker* section. The logic in `loader.js` is quite simple:

```
// ch8/ts/todo_webworkers/loader.ts
importScripts('/node_modules/systemjs/dist/system.src.js',
        '/node_modules/reflect-metadata/Reflect.js',
        '/node_modules/zone.js/dist/zone.js',
        './config.js');

System.import('./background_app.js')
.then(() => console.log('The application has started successfully'),
   error => console.error('error loading background', error));
```

As the first step, we import `SystemJS`, `ReflectMetadata` polyfils, `zone.js` and the configuration for `SystemJS`. Since this script is already run in WebWorkers, we have the `importScripts` method which allows us to load the listed files above. As last step we import the script which contains our application.

Now, let's explore how we bootstrap the application inside Web Worker:

```
import {bootstrapWorkerApp} from '@angular/platform-browser-dynamic';
// Logic for the application...
bootstrapWorkerApp(TodoApp).catch(err => console.error(err));
```

The preceding process is quite similar to what we are used to do when bootstrapping an Angular application running in the main UI thread. We import the method `bootstrapWorkerApp` and invoke it with the root component of our application as first argument.

Making an application compatible with Web Workers

As we said, the code that runs in the context of Web Worker does not have access to the DOM. Let's see what changes we need to make in order to address this limitation.

This is the original implementation of the `InputBox` component:

```
// ch4/ts/inputs-outputs/app.ts
@Component({
  selector: 'input-box',
  template: `
    <input #todoInput [placeholder]="inputPlaceholder">
    <button (click)="emitText(todoInput.value);
      todoInput.value = '';">
      {{buttonLabel}}
    </button>
  `
})
class InputBox {
  @Input() inputPlaceholder: string;
  @Input() buttonLabel: string;
  @Output() inputText = new EventEmitter<string>();
  emitText(text: string) {
    this.inputText.emit(text);
  }
}
```

Notice that inside the template, we named the input element `todoInput` and used its reference within the expression set as the handler of the click event. This code will not be able to run in Web Worker, since we directly access a DOM element inside the template. In order to take care of this, we need to refactor the snippet, so it uses Angular 2 bindings instead of directly touching any elements. We can either use inputs when a single direction binding makes sense or `NgModel` for achieving two-way data-binding, which is more computationally-intensive.

Let's use `NgModel`:

```
// ch8/ts/todo_webworkers/background_app.ts
import {NgModel} from '@angular/common';
@Component({
  selector: 'input-box',
  template: `
    <input [placeholder]="inputPlaceholder" [(ngModel)]="input">
    <button (click)="emitText()">
      {{buttonLabel}}
    </button>
  `
})
class InputBox {
  @Input() inputPlaceholder: string;
  @Input() buttonLabel: string;
  @Output() inputText = new EventEmitter<string>();
  input: string;
  emitText() {
    this.inputText.emit(this.input);
    this.input = '';
  }
}
```

In this version of the `InputBox` component, we will create a two-way data-binding between the input element and the input property of the `InputBox` component. Once the user clicks on the button, the `emitText` method will be invoked, which will trigger a new event emitted by `inputText EventEmitter`. In order to reset the value of the input element, we take advantage of the two-way data-binding that we declared and set the value of the input property to the empty string.

Moving the entire logic from the templates of the components to their controllers brings a lot of benefits, such as improved testability, maintainability, code reuse, and clarity.

The preceding code is compatible with the Web Workers environment, since the NgModel directive is based on an abstraction that does not manipulate the DOM directly, but instead, under the hood, exchanges messages asynchronously with the main UI thread.

To recap, we can say that while running applications in the context of Web Workers, we need to keep the following two things in mind:

- We need to use a different bootstrap process.
- We should not access the DOM directly.

Typical scenarios that violate the second point are as follows:

- Changing the DOM of the page by selecting an element and manipulating it directly with the browser's native APIs or a third-party library.
- Accessing native elements injected by using ElementRef.
- Creating a reference to an element in the template and passing it as an argument to methods.
- Directly manipulating an element referenced within the template.

In all these scenarios, we need to use the APIs provided by Angular. If we build our applications according to this practice, we will benefit not only from being able to run them in Web Workers, but also from increasing the code reuse in case we want to use them across different platforms.

Keeping this in mind will allow us to take advantage of server-side rendering.

Initial load of a single-page application

In this section, we will explore what server-side rendering is, why we need it in our applications, and how we can use it with Angular 2.

For our purposes, we'll explain the typical flow of events when a user opens a SPA implemented in Angular 2. First, we'll trace the events with the server-side rendering disabled, and after that, we'll see how we can benefit from this feature by enabling it. Our example will be illustrated in the context of HTTP 1.1.

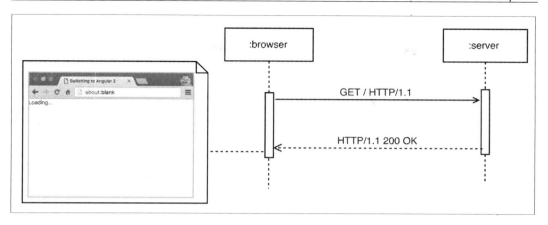

This image shows the first request by the browser and the corresponding server's response when loading a typical SPA. The result that the client will see initially is the initial content of the HTML page without any rendered components.

Let's suppose that we deploy the to-do application we built in *Chapter 4, Getting Started with Angular 2 Components and Directives* to a web server that has the `https://example.com` domain associated with it.

Once the user navigates to `https://example.com/`, the browser will open a new HTTP GET request, fetching the root resource (/). When the server receives the request, it will respond with an HTML file that, in our case, will look something like this:

```
<!DOCTYPE html>
<html lang="en">
<head>
  <title>Switching to Angular 2</title>
  <link rel="stylesheet" href="bootstrap.min.css">
</head>
<body>
  <app>Loading...</app>
  <script src="es6-shim.min.js"></script>
  <script src="Reflect.js"></script>
  <script src="system.src.js"></script>
  <script src="angular2-polyfills.js"></script>
  <script src="Rx.min.js"></script>
  <script src="angular2.js"></script>
  <script src="router.js"></script>
  <script src="http.min.js"></script>
  <script>...</script>
</body>
</html>
```

The browser will receive this content as the body of the response. When the markup is rendered onto the screen, all that the user will see is the label: **Loading....**.

In the next step, the browser will find all the references in the HTML file's external resources, such as styles and scripts, and start downloading them. In our case, some of them are `bootstrap.css`, `es6-shim.min.js`, `Reflect.js`, `system.src.js`, and `angular2-polyfills.js`.

Once all the referenced resources are available, there still won't be any significant visual progress for the user (except if the styles from the downloaded `css` file are applied to the page). This won't change until the JavaScript virtual machine processes all the referenced scripts related to the application's implementation. At this point, Angular will know which component needs to be rendered based on the current URL and bootstrap's configuration.

If the component associated with the page is defined in a separate file outside of our main application bundle, the framework will need to download it together with its entire dependency graph. In case the template and the styles of the component are externalized, Angular will need to download them as well before it is able to render the requested page.

Right after this, the framework will be able to compile the template associated with the target component and render the page.

In the previous scenario, there are the following two main pitfalls:

- Search engines are not that good at indexing dynamic content generated by JavaScript. This means that the **SEO** (**Search Engine Optimization**) of our SPA will suffer.
- In case of large applications and/or poor Internet connection, the user experience will be poor.

In the past, we solved the SEO issue in the applications built with AngularJS 1.x with different workarounds, such as using headless browser for rendering the requested page, caching it onto the disk, and later providing it to search engines. However, there's a more elegant solution.

Initial load of a SPA with server-side rendering

A couple of years ago, libraries such as `Rendr`, `Derby`, `Meteor`, and the others introduced the concept of isomorphic JavaScript applications, which were later renamed to universal. In essence, universal applications could be run on the client as well as on the server. Such portability is only possible in the case of low coupling between the SPA and the browser's APIs. The greatest benefit of this paradigm is that the application can be rerendered on the server and later sent to the client.

Universal applications are not framework-specific; we can take advantage of them in any framework that can be run outside of the environment of the browser. Conceptually, the practice of server-side rendering is very similar across platforms and libraries; only its implementation details may differ. For instance, the Angular 2 Universal module, which implements server-side rendering, has support for node.js as well as ASP.NET that, at the moment of this writing, is still work in progress.

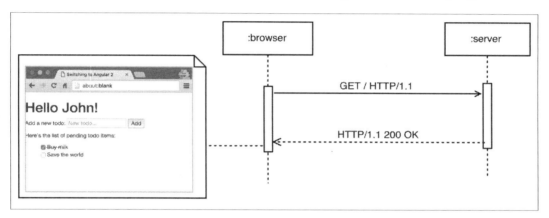

The preceding image shows the response by the server to the initial browser GET request. This time, in contrast to the typical scenario of loading a SPA, the browser will get the rendered content of the HTML page.

Let's trace the flow of the events in the same application with the server-side rendering feature enabled. In this case, once the server receives the HTTP GET request by the browser, it will run the SPA on the server in the node.js environment. All the DOM calls are going to be redirected to a server-side DOM implementation and be executed in the context of the used platform. Similarly, all the AJAX calls with the `http` module will be handled by the server-side implementation of the module. This way, the application will not make any difference, whether it is running in the context of the browser or the server.

Once the rendered version of the SPA is available, it can be serialized to HTML and sent to the browser. This time, during the application's initialization, instead of the **Loading...** label, the user will see the page they requested right away.

Note that at this point, the client will have the rendered version of the application, but all the referenced external resources, such as scripts and styles, still need to be available. This means that, initially, none of the CSS styles declared in the external files will be applied and the application will not be responsive to any user-related interactions, such as the mouse and keyboard events.

> Note that in case the scripts are inlined into the server-side rendered page, the application will be responsive to user events. However, inlining big chunks of JavaScript is generally considered as a bad practice, since it will increase the page's size dramatically and prevent the scripts from caching. Both will influence the network performance.

When the JavaScript virtual machine processes the JavaScript associated with the page, our SPA will be ready to use.

Server-side rendering with Angular 2

In the first half of 2015, Patrick Stapleton and Jeff Whelpley announced that they started the development of the module, **Universal**. Universal is a library that allows us to build universal (also called **isomorphic**) JavaScript applications with Angular 2; in other words, it provides server-side rendering support.

Applications built with Angular 2 and Universal will not be responsive until all the JavaScript belonging to the requested page is processed. This is a drawback that we already mentioned, which is valid for all the server-side rendered applications. However, Patrick and Jeff introduced **preboot.js**, which is a lightweight library that will be inlined on the page rendered by the server and available after the initial client request.

Preboot.js has several strategies for the management of the received client events before the application has been completely initialized. They are as follows:

- Record and play back events.
- Respond immediately to events.
- Maintain focus when a page is rerendered.
- Buffer client-side re-rendering for smoother transition.
- Freeze page until the bootstrap is complete if a user clicks on a button.

At the moment of this writing, the Universal module is still being actively developed. However, you can give it a try using the Angular 2 universal starter at `https://github.com/angular/universal-starter`.

Enhancing our development experience

Our experience as developers can be enhanced in terms of productivity or by allowing us to have more fun while working on our projects. This can be achieved with all the tools, IDEs, text editors, and more that we use on a daily basis. In this section, we'll briefly take a look at popular IDEs and text editors that we can use for taking advantage of the static code analysis features that Angular 2 provides.

In the second part of this section, we'll see what hot reloading is and how we can take advantage of it during the development of Angular 2 applications.

Text editors and IDEs

As we already mentioned at the beginning of the book, the core team put great effort into enhancing the tooling support in Angular 2. First of all, the framework is built with TypeScript, which naturally allows us to use static typing during our development process. Some of the text editors and IDEs that have great TypeScript support are as follows:

- **IntelliJ Idea**: A general-purpose IDE by JetBrains.
- **WebStorm**: An IDE specialized for web development by JetBrains.
- **VSCode**: A cross-platform text editor written in TypeScript and developed by Microsoft.
- **Sublime Text**: A cross-platform text editor.
- **Atom**: A cross-platform text editor.

Recently, JetBrains announced advanced Angular 2 support in IntelliJ Idea and WebStorm, which supports autocompletion for components and bindings.

Although not all the mentioned IDEs and text editors have Angular 2-specific support at the moment of this writing, Angular 2 comes with a great design. It allows us to perform advanced static code analysis on the application's codebase for the development of sophisticated refactoring and productivity tools in the near future. Until then, Angular 2 at least provides tooling support as good any other JavaScript framework in the market.

Hot reloading

Hot reloading (or hot loading) is a practice that got popular in the world of purely functional user interfaces in libraries such as Om (used with ClojureScript) and React.

When developing a SPA, it is quite annoying to refresh your browser after each small change of a style, view, or even a component. That's why a couple of years ago, a tool was developed called **livereload**. Livereload watches the files of our application, and when it detects a change in any of them, it sends a message to the browser to refresh the page. Usually, the connection established between the livereload server and the client is through WebSockets, since the server needs to send push notifications. Although this tool works great in some cases, it has one big disadvantage: once the page is refreshed, all of the state collected during the developer's interaction will be lost.

For instance, imagine a scenario where you're working on an application with a complex view. You navigate through a few pages, fill in forms, and set the values to input fields, and then, unexpectedly, you find an issue. You go to your text editor or IDE and fix the issue; the livereload server detects a change in your project's root and sends a notification to the browser in order to refresh the page. Now, you're back to the initial state of the application and you need to go through all these steps in order to reach the same point before the refresh.

In contrast to livereloading, in most cases, hot reloading can eliminate the state lost. Let's take a brief look at how it works.

A typical implementation of a hot reloader has two main modules: a client and a server. In contrast to the server in livereloading, the hot reloader server not only watches the file system for changes, but also takes the content of the changed file and sends it to the browser. Once the browser receives the message sent by the server, it can swap the previous implementation of the changed unit with the new one. After this, the view affected by the change can be rerendered in order to visually reflect the change. Since the application doesn't lose its state, we can continue from the point we've reached with the new version of the changed code unit.

Unfortunately, it is not always possible to dynamically swap the implementations of all your components using this strategy. If you update a piece of code that holds that holds application state, you may need to refresh the page manually.

Hot reloading in Angular 2

At the time of writing, there is a working prototype of Angular 2 hot reloader that can be tested with the angular2-seed described in the *Angular 2 quick starters* section. The project is in active development, so there are a lot of improvements on the roadmap. But it already provides its core functionality, which can ease the development experience significantly.

Bootstrapping a project with angular-cli

During AngularConnect 2015, Brad Green and Igor Minar, part of the Angular team, announced `angular-cli`—a CLI (command-line interface) tool to ease starting and managing Angular 2 applications. For those who have used Ruby on Rails, the idea behind the CLI tool might be familiar. The basic purpose of the tool is to allow the quick bootstrapping of new projects and scaffolding of new directives, components, pipes, and services.

At the time of writing, the tool is still in the early stage of development, so we'll demonstrate only its basic usage.

Using angular-cli

In order to install the CLI tool, run the following command in your terminal:

```
npm install -g angular-cli
```

Right after this, the global `ng` command will appear in your `$PATH`. For creating a new Angular 2 project, use the following:

```
# May take a while, depending on your Internet connection
ng new angular-cli-project
cd angular-cli project
ng serve
```

The preceding commands will do the following:

- Create a new Angular 2 project and install all of its node.js dependencies.
- Enter your project's directory.
- Start a development web server that will let you open the application you just created in your web browser.

For further reading, take a look at the project's repository located at `https://github.com/angular/angular-cli`.

Angular 2 quick starters

Although Angular 2 CLI is going to be amazing, at the moment of this writing, it is still at a very early stage of development. It's build-tool agnostic, which means that it doesn't provide any build system. Luckily, there are a lot of starter projects developed by the community that can provide a great starting point for our next Angular 2 project.

Angular 2 seed

In case you enjoy Gulp and static typing, you can give a try to the angular2-seed project. It is hosted on GitHub at the following URL: `https://github.com/mgechev/angular2-seed`.

The Angular 2 seed provides the following key features:

- Advanced, ready-to-go, easy-to-extend, modular, and statically typed build system using Gulp.
- Production and development builds.
- Integration with Angular Mobile Toolkit.
- Sample unit tests with Jasmine and Karma.
- End-to-end tests with Protractor.
- A development server with Livereload.
- Experimental hot reloading support.
- Following the best practices for your applications' and files' organization.
- Manager for the TypeScript-related type definitions.

The code distributed with the book is based on this seed project.

For angular2-seed, you need to have node.js, npm, and Git installed, and you need to run the following list of commands:

```
git clone --depth 1 https://github.com/mgechev/angular2-seed.git
cd angular2-seed
npm install
npm start
```

After you run these commands, your browser will be automatically opened with the home page of the seed. On the change of any of the TypeScript files, the code will be automatically transpiled to JavaScript and your browser will be refreshed.

The production build is configurable, but by default, it produces a single bundle that contains a minified version of the application and all the referenced libraries.

Angular 2 Webpack starter

If you prefer declarative and minimalistic builds with Webpack, you can use *angular2-webpack-starter*. It is a starter project developed by *AngularClass* and hosted on GitHub. You can find it at the following URL: `https://github.com/AngularClass/angular2-webpack-starter`.

This starter provides the following features:

- The best practices in file and application organization for Angular 2.
- Ready-to-go build system using Webpack for working with TypeScript.
- Testing Angular 2 code with Jasmine and Karma.
- Coverage with Istanbul and Karma.
- End-to-end Angular 2 code using Protractor.
- Type manager with Typings.

In order to give it a try, you need to have node.js, npm, and git installed, and you need to run the following commands:

```
git clone --depth 1 https://github.com/angularclass/angular2-webpack-starter.git
cd angular2-webpack-starter
npm install
./node_modules/.bin/typings install
npm start
```

Summary

We started this book by introducing the reasons behind the development of Angular 2, which was followed by a conceptual overview that gave us a general idea about the building blocks that the framework provides for application development. In the next step, we did a TypeScript crash course that prepared us for *Chapter 4*, *Getting Started with Angular 2 Components and Directives* where we went deep into Angular's directives, components, and change detection.

In *Chapter 5*, *Dependency Injection in Angular 2* we explained the dependency injection mechanism and saw how we can manage the relations between the different components by using it. The next chapters explained to us how we can build forms and pipes, and take advantage of Angular 2's component-based router.

By completing the current chapter, we finished our journey into the framework. At the moment of this writing, the design decisions and the ideas behind Angular 2's core are solid and finalized. Although the framework is still brand new, in the past couple of months its ecosystem reached a level that we can develop production-ready, high-performance, SEO-friendly applications, and on top of this, have a great development experience exploiting static typing and hot reloading.

Index

Symbol

@RouteConfig
used, for route configuration 161, 162

A

access modifiers
private 61
protected 61
public 60
ambient type definitions
custom 71, 72
predefined ambient type definitions,
    using 69-71
d.ts files, defining 72, 73
using 69
**AMD (Asynchronous Module
    Definition) 50**
Angular 2
about 224
and Web Workers 211
AsyncPipe, using 206
built-in directives, using 90, 91
built-in pipes, using 202
components 23, 24
conceptual overview 16-18
Dependency Injection (DI) 128
Gulp seed 224
Hello world! application, building 76-78
hot reloading 223
HTTP module, exploring 191
HTTP module, using 193, 194
index, defining 81
model-driven forms, developing 186
playing with 80, 81

route, definition syntax 36, 37
Webpack starter 225
Angular 2 directives
constructor, defining 88, 89
defining 86, 87
encapsulation 89, 90
inputs, setting 88
ngFor directive 84
using 82, 83
Angular 2 forms
built-in form validators, using 171
custom control validators, defining 172-174
data, storing 181
model-driven approach 167
NgForm directive, using 176-178
select inputs, using 174, 175
template-driven forms, developing 168
template-driven form's markup,
    exploring 170, 171
used, for two-way data-binding 179-181
using 167
Angular 2 router
application, bootstrapping 159, 160
exploring 158
lazy-loading, with AsyncRoute 164-167
PathLocationStrategy, using 160
root component, defining 159, 160
routerLink, using 162
router-outlet, using 162, 163
routes, configuring with @RouteConfig 161
angular2-seed project
URL 224
angular-cli
URL 223
used, for bootstrapping project 223

AngularJS 1.x
about 6
change detection 13, 28, 29
change detection, enhancing 30, 31
controllers 6, 7
Dependency Injection (DI) 8
scope object 7, 8
server-side rendering 9
single-page applications 10, 11
templates 11, 12
application
migrating, to Web Worker 212-214
running, in Web Workers,
bootstrapping 211, 212
AsyncPipe
using 206, 207
using, with observables 207
AsyncRoute
used, for lazy-loading 164-167

B

block scope
used, for defining variables 47
built-in change detection
dynamic change detection 13
JIT change detection 13
built-in form validators
maxlength 171
minlength 171
using 171
built-in pipes
AsyncPipe 202
CurrencyPipe 202
DatePipe 202
DecimalPipe 202
JsonPipe 202
LowerCasePipe 202
PercentPipe 202
SlicePipe 202
UpperCasePipe 202
using 202

C

change detection
about 13, 17, 27
defining 118

enhancing 118
enhancing, in AngularJS 1.x 30, 31
example 27
immutable data structures, using
in Angular 123, 124
in AngularJS 1.x 28, 29
in zone.js 30
order of execution 119, 120
performance boosting, with immutable
data and OnPush 122, 123
simplified data-flow 30
strategies 121
child injectors
about 138, 139
dependencies, configuring 140
element injectors 146, 147
Coders repository application
bootstrapping 159
developing 156, 157
views 156
CommonJS 50
component-based router
about 35, 36
Angular 2 route, definition syntax 36, 37
Component class 22
components
about 16, 21
composing 22, 23
Dependency Injection (DI),
exploring with 148
Dependency Injection (DI), using 145, 146
in Angular 2, 23, 24
Composite class 21
container 130
content children 106
content projection, Angular 2
about 103
components, nesting 105, 106
ContentChildren, using 106-108
defining 102
multiple content chunks, projecting 104
ViewChildren, using 106-108
ViewChild, versus ContentChild 108-111
controller as syntax 7
controllers 6, 7
control validators
composition, using 189, 190

Create Retrieve Update and
    Delete (CRUD) 167
CSP (Content-Security-Policy) 118
CSS classes
    about 171
    ng-dirty 171
    ng-invalid 171
    ng-pristine 171
    ng-touched 171
    ng-untouched 171
    ng-valid 171
custom control validators
    defining 172-174

D

data
    transforming, pipes used 200
decorators
    URL 48
DefinitelyTyped
    URL 69
dependencies, child injectors
    configuring 140
    multiproviders, using 144, 145
    optional dependencies, using 142, 143
    self decorator, using 140
    self injector, skipping 141
Dependency Injection (DI)
    about 8, 16, 127
    benefits 128, 129
    exploring, with components 148
    in Angular 2 128
    need for 127, 128
    using, with components and
        directives 145, 146
    using, with ES5 151-153
differs 17
directives
    about 16
    Dependency Injection (DI), using 145, 146
    modifying 18-20
directives syntax
    semantics, defining 84, 85
    syntax sugar used, in templates 86
    variables, declaring inside template 85
Domain Specific Language (DSL) 11, 20, 151

dynamic change detection 13

E

ECMAScript
    evolution 3
    Web Components 3, 4
    WebWorkers 4, 5
ECMAScript 5 (ES5)
    about 19
    Dependency Injection (DI), using 151-153
ECMAScript 2015 (ES2015)
    about 2
    aliases, using 52
    and ES2016 classes, using 45, 47
    and ES2016, recap 54
    arrow functions 44, 45
    default exports 52
    implicit asynchronous behavior 52
    modular code, writing with 50
    module exports, importing 52
    module loader 53, 54
    module syntax, using 51
    TypeScript features 43
    TypeScript syntax 43
element injectors
    about 146, 147
    Dependency Injection (DI), exploring
        with components 148
    providers, declaring 147, 148
    viewProviders, versus providers 148-150
Enum types 56
environment, Angular 2
    project repository, installing 79
    references 79
    setting up 79
    URL, for issues 80
ES2016 decorators
    configurable decorators, using 49, 50
    meta-programming with 48, 49

F

factories
    defining, for instantiating services 136-138
    using 136
forward references 132, 133

G

generic code
  generic functions, using 67
  multiple type parameters, having 67
  writing, type parameters used 65-67
generic views
  defining, with TemplateRef 116-118
GitHub API token
  reference link 192
Google Closure Compiler 40

H

Hello world! application
  defining, in Angular 2 76-78
host injectors 146-148
hot reloading
  about 222
  in Angular 2 223
HTTP module
  exploring 191, 192
  using 193

I

IDEs 221
injector
  about 129
  child injectors 138, 139
  configuring 129, 130
  dependency resolution, with generated
     metadata 130, 131
  factories, defining for instantiating
     services 136-138
  factories, using 136
  forward references 132, 133
  hierarchy, building 139, 140
  instantiating 131, 132
  providers, configuring 134
inline caching
  reference link 13
interfaces
  about 63, 64
  inheritance 64
  multiple interfaces, implementing 64
inversion of control (IoC) 8
isomorphic 220

J

JIT change detection 13

L

Leaf class 21
less verbose code
  best common type 68
  contextual type inference 69
  writing, with TypeScript's type inference 68
lifecycle, component
  hooking into 112, 113
livereload 222

M

Massive View Controller (MVC) 7
model-driven forms, Angular 2
  control validators composition,
     using 189, 190
  developing 186-188
Model View Controller (MVC) 6, 21
Model View Presenter (MVP) 6
Model View ViewModel (MVVM) 6, 21
Model View Whatever (MVW) 6, 27
multiproviders
  using 144, 145

N

nested routes
  defining 197-200
NgForm directive
  using 176-179
node.js
  URL 42
Node Package Manager (npm)
  used, for installing TypeScript 42
nvm
  URL 79

O

object-oriented (OO) paradigm 45
Object types
  Array types 57, 58
  Function types 58, 59

operation 22
order of execution
   tracing 114, 115

P

parameterized views
   defining 195, 196
PathLocationStrategy
   using 160
pipes
   about 17, 25
   built-in pipes, using 202
   defining 25, 26
   stateful pipes, developing 203, 204
   stateless pipes, developing 200, 201
   used, for data transformations 200
preboot.js 220
primitive types 56
providers
   about 129
   configuring 134
   declaring, for element injectors 147, 148
   existing providers, using 135
   versus viewProviders 148-150

R

root component
   defining 159
route
   definition syntax 36, 37
routerLink
   using 162, 163
router-outlet
   using 163
RxJS GitHub repository
   about 76
   URL 76

S

scope object 7, 8
Search Engine Optimization (SEO)
   about 9
   and UI 218
select inputs
   using, with Angular 2 forms 174, 175

self decorator
   using 140
self injector
   skipping 141
server-side rendering 9
services
   about 18, 32-35
   instantiating, with factories 136-138
single-page application
   about 10, 11, 35, 209
   initial load 216, 218
   initial load, with enabled server-side
      rendering 219, 220
   server-side rendering, with Angular 2 220
stateful pipes
   developing 203, 204
   using 205, 206
stateless pipes
   developing 200, 201
static typing
   about 54
   access modifiers, using 60-62
   Array types 57, 58
   classes, defining 60
   Enum types 56
   explicit type definitions, using 55
   Function types 58, 59
   interface inheritance 64
   interfaces, defining 63, 64
   multiple interfaces, implementing 64, 65
   Object types 57
   primitive types 56
   type any 55
stored developers
   listing 182, 183
subtyping 63

T

template-driven forms
   developing 167-169
   markup, exploring 169-171
TemplateRef
   generic views, defining with 116-118
templates 11, 12
text editors
   and IDEs 221

time to live (TTL) 10
Todo application
  components 95, 96
  component's controllers,
      implementing 91-93
token 129, 130
transpilation 3
Transport Layer Security (TLS) 136
two-way data-binding
  using, with Angular 2 179-181
type inference
  used, for writing less verbose code 68
type parameters
  generic functions, using 67
  multiple type parameters, having 67
  used, for writing generic code 65-67
TypeScript
  about 39, 40
  benefits 41
  compile-time type checking 40
  decorators 65
  ES2015 and ES2016 classes, using 45-47
  ES2015 arrow functions 44, 45
  features, by ES2015 and ES2016 43
  index, defining 81
  installing, npm used 42
  playing with 80, 81
  program, running 43
  syntax, by ES2015 and ES2016 43
  text editors and IDEs, support 40, 41
  using 42, 78
  variables, defining with block scope 47
types, TypeScript
  about 55
  object types 56
  primitive types 56
  type parameters 56
  union types 56

U

Universal 220
universal starter
  URL 221
user actions
  alternative syntax, for defining input and
      output 102

component's input and output,
    defining 96-98
directives' input and output, finding
    out 95, 96
directives' input and output, using 94
event bubbling 100
handling 93, 94
input and output of directive,
    renaming 100, 101
input, passing 98-100
output, consuming 98-100

V

view children 106
view encapsulation, component
  defining 91
viewProviders
  versus providers 148-150
views, Coders repository application
  basic details 156

W

Web
  evolution 2
Web Components
  about 2
  evolution 3, 4
Webpack starter
  URL 225
Web Workers API
  about 210
  and Angular 2 211
  and UI 212
  application, bootstrapping 211, 212
  application, migrating to 212-214
  applications, running 209, 210
  compatible, application creating 214-216
WebWorkers 2-5

Z

zone.js
  change detection 30